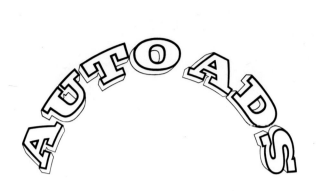

Also by Jane Stern

*Trucker: A Portrait of the Last American Cowboy*

Also by Jane and Michael Stern

*Amazing America*
*Roadfood*

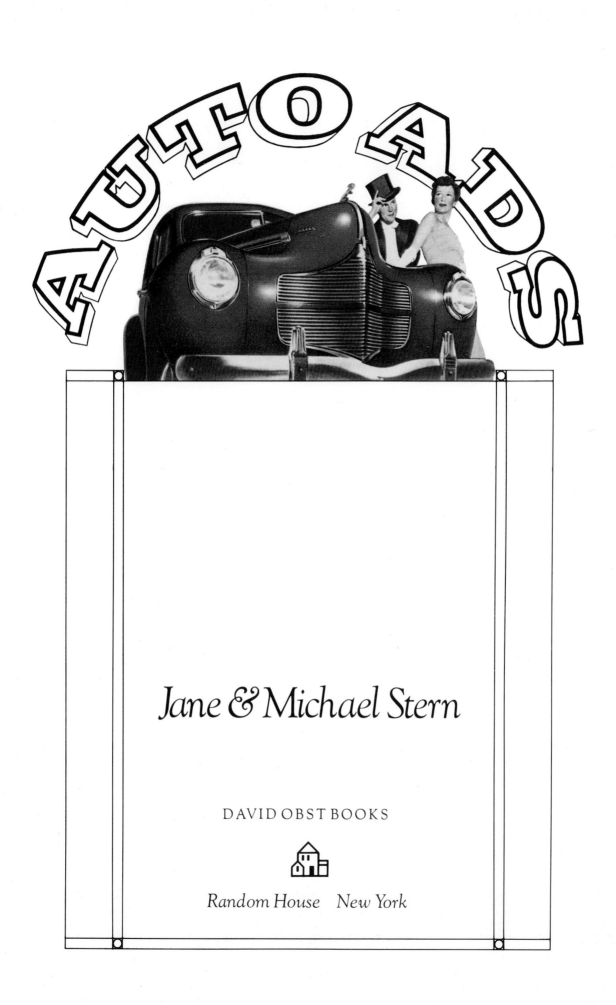

# AUTO ADS

Jane & Michael Stern

DAVID OBST BOOKS

Random House   New York

## Acknowledgments

We would like to express our gratitude to Kathy Matthews, David Obst, and Betty Anne Clarke for the encouragement and interest they offered throughout the completion of this project.

Invaluable assistance was provided by Eugene Richmond of American Motors; Skip Marketti of the Auburn-Cord-Duesenberg Museum; Bob Bastress, photographer; Bob Burden of British-Leyland; George Frink of Buick; Gary Bell and Norbert Bartos of Cadillac; Amber McCoy of Campbell-Ewald; Cynthia Chambers and Carl Krampert of D'Arcy-MacManus & Masius; Jim Sponseller of Fisher Body; Thomas J. Mullen of General Motors; J. Peter Scherer of the Jeep Corporation; Robert W. Irelan and Janet Mangini of Kaiser Industries; Hal Randall of McCann-Erickson; Otto Merte and Jim Wren of the Motor Vehicle Manufacturers Association; John MacDonald of Nissan Motors; Helen Earley of Oldsmobile; Jerry Sherman of Scali, McCabe, Sloves; Mary Gegelys of J. Walter Thompson; and Renay Immel and John Slaven of Volkswagen.

Special thanks are due J. B. McMechan of Ford for his help and hospitality during our stay in Dearborn; Harry Stern for his photographic assistance; and Stan Yost, who generously shared with us his extensive archives and knowledge of automobile history.

Library of Congress Cataloging in Publication Data
Stern, Jane.
Auto ads.
1.   Advertising—Automobile industry and trade.
2.   United States—Social conditions.   I.   Stern, Michael,
1946–       joint author.   II.   Title.
HF6161.A   659.1′9′629222   78-57139
ISBN 0-394-50094-6

Manufactured in the United States of America
24689753
First Edition

*Designed by Bernard Klein*

*This book is dedicated to Reverend Howard Finster*

YOUR point of view of motoring is determined by the car you own: pleasure and comfort are dependent on its year-in-and-year-out reliability. Riding in an

# OLDSMOBILE

the machinery is only apparent as an unobtrusive source of power—boundless, yet delightfully responsive. Inevitably the Oldsmobile owner learns to place absolute confidence in his car . . . . and <u>he</u> experiences the real pleasure of motoring.

Four-cylinder cars $2750.    Closed bodies for each chassis.
Six-cylinder cars $4500.     Details sent on request.

## OLDS MOTOR WORKS

Lansing, Mich.

Oldsmobile Co. of Canada, Limited, 80 King St., East Toronto, Ont.

1904

# 1900     1910

*A man drove his Cadillac up the steps of the
Capitol at Washington. He paid for his fun,
but it was worth the money to know
the power of the Cadillac.*

—CADILLAC AD, 1904

"**B**ully" was the way Teddy Roosevelt described the mood at the turn of the century. Red, white and blue Centennial heraldry ushered in a decade of hard work, romantic idealism, and high spirits. It was a time when immigrants teemed into Ellis Island. The very rich built golden castles on the sandy banks of Newport. And the middle class grew, as people left their small towns and farms and headed toward the city to seek their fortune.

In 1900 the average man took home a paycheck of $12.74 for a 59-hour workweek. There were 17.6 phones for every 1,000 Americans. The airplane had not yet been built. And there were less than 150 miles of paved road for the country's 8,000 automobiles. Of course, they weren't all called automobiles. Nobody was quite sure *what* to call them. Among the choices were these: autobat, autocycle, autogo, self-motor, farmobile, pneumobile, zentmobile, and ipsometer. "Horseless carriage" had been popular through the last years of the nineteenth century. A local Boston exhibition of the machines was called a Motor Carriage Exhibition. In Madison Square Garden in 1900 the first major presentation was called the National Automobile Show, and the name seemed to stick.

The fact is, early automobiles were little more than carriages without the horse. The autocar boasted that it was "simple as a pair of reins" (1905). Early in the century a U.S. patent was given for a motor-powered vehicle with wheels hidden inside the "hooves" of a full-size metal "horse" that contained an engine to pull the carriage behind. Paul Wilson, in his book *Chrome Dreams*, suggests that the development of a hood, or boxlike section, in front of the early runabouts was not for housing the engine (which was underneath the carriage), but was rather "a symbolic substitute for the horse, an easily recognized symbol of power."

In an effort to prove that the automobile was superior to the horse, early advertisers compared the two and, of course, found the old nag lacking. Oldsmobile told "A Tale of Two Streets" (1904), which contrasted a muddy, grubby street populated by a lonely horse to the paved, bustling boulevard on which rode the Olds—a far more appealing tableau.

Motoring required mechanical skills or the employment of a full-time mechanic. It was an adventure, and it called for special tools. Hammacher Schlemmer offered a "tourist autokit" in 1906. It weighed eighteen pounds and contained thirty-eight wrenches and screwdrivers. But was that enough? One certainly needed a vulcanizer to repair flats and a gas can when you had to hunt for fuel. In 1908 the C.A.C. Axe Company asked: "Did it ever occur to you that the Damascus Hatchet would be a mighty convenient and dependable acquisition to the auto tool chest? When the wheel drops out of sight in the mud, get out the Damascus, cut a pole for a lever, right things up, and then on your way again." The Saks & Co. Emergency Motorist Kit included four pounds of meat, two pounds of chocolate, and hardtack—enough to keep you alive until old dobbin pulled you out of the ditch.

Special clothing for automobile travel was a necessity. Goggles, caps, turbans, veils, and furs were designed to protect against the elements. For winter wear there were body bags lined with nutria or wombat fur, foot muffs, and one item known as the "neck, ear, and chest muffler"—an all-in-one wraparound mummy bag.

Not every motorist had to worry about maneuvering through ditches and mud. Perhaps his motorcar was simply for pleasure-driving around the grounds of an elegant estate. The automobile had become the new status mount, and the very rich of the era, such as the Vanderbilts and the Goulds, maintained stables of them. What they might spend on a Great Arrow or Packard was what any normal family would have to pay for a six-room house with all the furnishings.

Even the early Fords (which cost between $800 and $2,000 in 1905) were advertised as vehicles to be driven by one's chauffeur. In 1906 Woodrow Wilson (then president of Princeton University) warned: "Nothing has spread socialistic feeling in this country more than the use of the automobile. To the country man, they are a picture of the arrogance of wealth, with all its independence and carelessness."

But Wilson misread the feelings of upwardly striving America. In this era of pluck and luck, Horatio Alger and square-jawed Frank Merriwell were the heroes. Hard work and ingenuity were a sure path not only to success but to its new hallmark—the automobile.

Professional men bought cars. "Doctors, lawyers, merchants," Oldsmobile proclaimed in 1904. "You see them everywhere." In fact, doctors were among the first non-bluebloods to take to the automobile. In 1906 the *Journal of the American Medical Association* published a special issue called "Autos for Physicians." Cadillac declared its coupe to be "The Ideal Physician's Car" (1906) because it was comfortable in any weather. Cars were especially handy for house calls, since their headlights could be shined in the window to provide light for operations.

When the middle-class family did obtain a car, it was most likely a pleasure vehicle. To cries of "Get a horse!" they sputtered and bounced along dirt paths or through fields or down city boulevards. There were automobile clubs, motorized hunting parties, and cross-country journeys. Of course, there were no road maps, but occasionally there were "picto-maps," with photographs illustrating turns and stops along the way.

Obstacles to happy motoring included ridiculous regulations. The State of Tennessee demanded one week's notice before leaving on a motor trip. Vermont declared that autos were to be preceded by a "mature individual" waving a red flag.

Despite the hardships, cars became a national craze. "In My Merry Oldsmobile" was the most popular song of 1905. The car became a source of vaudeville jokes and popular humor. It even nabbed a starring role in a melodrama called *The Great Automobile Mystery*. America was infatuated with the automobile and its adventuresome possibilities. Its very existence expressed the forward movement of the country; and although it would have many enemies to battle along the way, by 1910 there could be no doubt that the slim, black, backfiring beauty was here to stay.

1901

## AUTOMOBILES 66

### The **FORD** MOTOR CAR

## In the eyes of the Chauffeur

is the most satisfactory Automobile made for every-day service. The two-cylinder (opposed) motor gives 8 actual horse-power, and eliminates the vibration so noticeable in other machines. The body is luxurious and comfortable and can be removed from the chassis by loosening six bolts.

**Price with Tonneau $900.00**
**As a Runabout      $800.00**

Standard equipment includes 3-inch heavy double-tube tires

We agree to assume all responsibility in any action the TRUST may take regarding alleged infringement of the Selden Patent to prevent you from buying the Ford—"*The Car of Satisfaction.*"

### We Hold the World's Record.

The Ford "999" (the fastest machine in the world), driven by Mr. Ford, made a mile in 39⅖ seconds; equal to 92 miles an hour.

Write for illustrated catalogue and name of our nearest agent.

## Ford Motor Co., Detroit, Mich.

**Bringing in The Yule Log**

# The Oldsmobile

No roads too rough or uneven for the Olds-mobile. Its strong construction and simple mechanism are built to undergo the most severe usage. Its easy, cushioned frame affords perfect comfort to its occupants at all times. Embodying the latest improvements that our long experience has suggested, the Oldsmobile is to-day, in all seasons and on all roads, "the best thing on wheels."

For stormy weather, the Oldsmobile can be fitted with a waterproof top and apron that provides perfect protection for the occupants and the operating lever.

Selling agencies in all the large cities, or write for full information to Department G.

OLDS MOTOR WORKS, DETROIT, U.S.A.
Member of the Association of Licensed Automobile Manufacturers.

8-88 ROADSTER $1995

*80 Miles Per Hour*     *130 Inch Wheelbase*
*Five Passenger Capacity*     *Door for Rear Seat*

*6-66, $1095 to $1345  8-77, $1395 to $1745  8-88, $1995 to $2595  Freight, Tax and Equipment Extra*

AUBURN AUTOMOBILE COMPANY, AUBURN, INDIANA

# AVBVRN

*1927*

# 1910  1930

*Lighter than any on the road, . . . rare in
beauty and supremely balanced . . . the Playboy
is apt companion for all Americans who dare
never to grow old.*

—JORDAN PLAYBOY AD, MID-TWENTIES

"**I**'m going to build a car for the masses," said Henry Ford in 1903. Five years later he kept his promise by producing what was advertised as "the universal car," the Model T. It was the beginning of the automobile age.

The Model T was simple, easy to fix, and unstoppable. Its strength and reliability became the stuff of popular mythology. Around 1910 Lizzie was the nickname for hard-working, loyal domestic servants. Lizzies were expected to be available for any chores their masters or mistresses might devise—and so it was with the versatile Model T. Used for everything from a motorized plow to a church on wheels, it was soon affectionately tagged "the tin Lizzie."

America fell in love with Henry Ford's car. It opened new vistas for people who would never have thought of buying a car. It was embraced wholly—for its shortcomings as well as its charms. The Ford was a national fad, and pretty soon the country was telling "Ford jokes":

The Ford is the best family car. It has a tank for father, a hood for mother, and a rattle for baby.

A dying man had one request—to be buried with his Model T. He had never yet been in a hole where his Ford couldn't pull him out.

"What shock absorbers do you use on that Ford?" "The passengers."

By 1920 half of the eight million cars on the road were Model Ts. There had been nothing comparable throughout the teens. Year-to-year standardization drove the cost to below $300. The Ford was the product of a conservative, thrifty era. Buying one was like putting money into a savings account. The return was reliable if unspectacular. But as a new decade began, America was learning to live on the installment plan.

After the war it was "Buy now, pay later." Anything old was discarded, and in its place emerged "the new woman," "the new morality," "the new science," and a new magazine called *The New Yorker*, announcing itself as "Not for the old lady from Dubuque." Fads ignited like comets, and just as quickly burned themselves out. There was mah-jongg, crossword puzzles, Lucky Lindy soaring over the ocean, Leopold and Loeb, the Scopes trial, and "Yes, We Have No Bananas." Everything *new* was embraced for the moment. Modern equaled good or, at least, exciting.

In this era of short skirts and short hair, flesh-colored stockings, and rouge for both knees and cheeks, the old Tin Lizzie began to look like a dowdy relic. One of the decade's faddish heroes among intellectuals was Sigmund Freud, whose complex theories were popularized as a blunt exhortation to be uninhibited, to express sexuality. The conservative, monotone Model T was hardly the vehicle in which to drive into the new, hot-blooded era of the freed libido. However dependable or cheap it was, Henry Ford's car did not have "it."

The 1925 Chevrolet did. What it had was a brightly colored Duco finish, front and rear bumpers, a shiny radiator, and wheel disks painted to match the car. In 1927 Chevrolet's parent company, General Motors, organized an Art and Color Division to work exclusively on car appearance. That same year, with Chevrolet sales figures way out in front, Model T production ceased. The Universal Car was a thing of the past.

Reliability was no longer enough. A car had to fit into the colorful wonderland of material goods that were making modern life so exciting. There seemed to be an unquenchable desire for radios, refrigerators, movies and movie palaces. The comfortable closed car, which in 1919 comprised only 10 percent of all car sales, leaped to 83 percent of the market by 1927. Motoring was no longer an adventure. It was an everyday pleasure, just one happy result of prosperity.

The comfort of the new automobile was greeted with some moral outrage. Historian Frederick Lewis Allen noted, in *Only Yesterday:* "The closed car was in effect a room protected from the weather which could be occupied any time of the day or night and could be moved at will into a darkened byway or country lane." In a 1929 study of American culture,

*Middletown*, the town judge called the auto "a house of prostitution on wheels."

Along with the raccoon coat and hip flask, the auto became a symbol of flaming youth. The young generation was both deified and vilified during the 1920s, and the speed at which it lived was supplied by the automobile. Cars were thought to contribute not only to promiscuity but to coeducational drinking.

The car also became a symbol of lawlessness—the bootlegger's tool and the gangster's shield. Wherever Al Capone went, he traveled in a procession of three cars—one in front to clear the way, one in back filled with armed guards, and his own armor-plated McFarland limousine in the middle. A new, satanic mythology grew up around the automobile, deliverer of bombs, harbinger of machine-gun bullets, and grim carrier for the one-way ride.

More mundane problems arose with the new auto-mobility. There were no highways and few major bridges. On a summer weekend night, the trip from New Jersey to New York took several hours—waiting behind hundreds of cars for the cross-Hudson ferry. The traffic jam was born.

America began to talk of "Sunday drivers." Roadside stands, gas stations, and tourist courts appeared on the landscape. Camping became a national fad. The first mobile home was built in 1929—and sold to Henry Ford. The car was the instrument of a new freedom as the newly coined expression "See America first" became a reality to millions.

Automobile production had become the lifeblood of 1920s prosperity. But for business to prosper, the consumer had to buy more and more. It became the job of advertising not merely to tell of a product but to create a need. And so magazine advertisements brought to their readers not merely seductive promises but anxiety-producing sagas of woe. Copywriters had a field day manufacturing modern folk tales such as the woman who stayed at home because her B.O. drove away her suitors and the salesman who couldn't make the deal because his halitosis repelled the buyer. All these dilemmas could of course be solved—by purchasing the appropriate product.

Auto ads seldom resorted to such unabashed melodrama, but they did make some fancy promises:

> *By stimulating good health and efficiency, owning a Ford increases your earning power.*
>
> —Ford ad, 1924

> SOMETHING EXTRA FROM LIFE. . . . *There is waiting for you in a Buick more satisfaction than you have ever known.*
>
> —Buick ad, 1925

The new woman—who might be earning a living herself, and who was freed from old-fashioned housework by the growing availability of canned goods, washing machines, and vacuum cleaners—was a ready target for the car makers. Even if she did not buy the car, Henry Ford figured, she made up her husband's mind, and so almost all Ford ads during the twenties were directed at women.

Mechanical reliability and strength were virtues that took a back seat to pleasure, freedom, comfort, and style. Soft hues and delicate phraseology replaced nuts-and-bolts information. The car buyer was not buying a piece of machinery. He or she was buying a new life.

> *Buick spreads a magic carpet of better transportation from where you are to where you want to be.*
>
> —Buick ad, 1928

The ultimate expression of the intangible benefits of car ownership was Cadillac's "Penalty of Leadership" ad of 1915. With Olympian detachment, the copy never stoops to mention the car. But the point was clearly made. The buyer of a Cadillac partook of greatness.

It was Ned Jordan who perfected the dreamy poetry of advertising copy. His "Somewhere West of Laramie" is the classic, but there were others, equally lyrical:

> *Somewhere far beyond the place where men and women and motors race through the canyons of the town—somewhere on the top of the world—there is a peak which dull care has never climbed. You can go there lighthearted in a Jordan Playboy—for it's always happy in the hills.*

The snob appeal of Jordan's ads was not always so implicit:

> *Strangely we have always underestimated the Playboy demand. We have never built enough. But we never will—you may be assured. There's too much fun in building a few less than the people want. It's friendly, human—you know—to want to have something the other fellow can't get.*

By the end of the twenties the rich were getting very much richer. Custom car designers and luxury models were thriving. The clutter of facts and information was brushed aside for the salient phrase and telling illustration. "Ask the man who owns one" was all that was needed to promote the Packard. The V-16 Cadillac was announced under a headline that read "Works of the Modern Masters." "He Drives a Duesenberg" appeared in the early thirties—well into the depression—under drawings of gentlemen who obviously had no concern about the plummeting economy, nor for things mechanical, practical, or automotive.

"To hell with mechanical chatter," Ned Jordan had said. By the end of the decade, it was *design* and *image* that sold cars. Even Ford had replaced the Model T with the more fashionable and mechanically modern Model A. Car manufacturers stood at the brink of the streamlined decade—a classical era in which mechanical design and flowing form were wed as the culmination of the machine age.

## THE PENALTY OF LEADERSHIP

IN EVERY field of human endeavor, he that is first must perpetually live in the white light of publicity. Whether the leadership be vested in a man or in a manufactured product, emulation and envy are ever at work. ℂ In art, in literature, in music, in industry, the reward and the punishment are always the same. ℂ The reward is widespread recognition; the punishment, fierce denial and detraction. ℂ When a man's work becomes a standard for the whole world, it also becomes a target for the shafts of the envious few. If his work be merely mediocre, he will be left severely alone—if he achieve a masterpiece, it will set a million tongues a-wagging. ℂ Jealousy does not protrude its forked tongue at the artist who produces a commonplace painting. ℂ Whatsoever you write, or paint, or play, or sing, or build, no one will strive to surpass or to slander you, unless your work be stamped with the seal of genius. ℂ Long, long after a great work or a good work has been done, those who are disappointed or envious continue to cry out that it cannot be done. ℂ Spiteful little voices in the domain of art were raised against our own Whistler as a mountebank, long after the big world had acclaimed him its greatest artistic genius. ℂ Multitudes flocked to Bayreuth to worship at the musical shrine of Wagner, while the little group of those whom he had dethroned and displaced argued angrily that he was no musician at all. ℂ The little world continued to protest that Fulton could never build a steamboat, while the big world flocked to the river banks to see his boat steam by. ℂ The leader is assailed because he is a leader, and the effort to equal him is merely added proof of that leadership. ℂ Failing to equal or to excel, the follower seeks to depreciate and to destroy—but only confirms once more the superiority of that which he strives to supplant. ℂ There is nothing new in this. It is as old as the world and as old as the human passions—envy, fear, greed, ambition, and the desire to surpass. ℂ And it all avails nothing. ℂ If the leader truly leads, he remains—the leader. ℂ Master-poet, master-painter, master-workman, each in his turn is assailed, and each holds his laurels through the ages. ℂ That which is good or great makes itself known, no matter how loud the clamor of denial. ℂ That which deserves to live—lives.

1915

Her habit of measuring time in terms of dollars gives the woman in business keen insight into the true value of a Ford closed car for her personal use.

This car enables her to conserve minutes, to expedite her affairs, to widen the scope of her activities. Its low first cost, long life and inexpensive operation and upkeep convince her that it is a sound investment value.

And it is such a pleasant car to drive that it transforms the business call which might be an interruption into an enjoyable episode of her busy day.

TUDOR SEDAN, $590          FORDOR SEDAN, $685          COUPE, $525          (All prices f. o. b. Detroit)

*Ford*
CLOSED CARS

## for the
### YOUNG BUSINESS MAN

The Ford Runabout is a profitable partner and a happy companion for the boy who is making his mark in business and at school.

It reduces distance from a matter of miles to a matter of minutes. By saving time and effort, it makes larger earnings possible. And costing little to buy and keep going, it quickly pays for itself.

When vacation time rolls round the Runabout enables the young business man to reduce by hours the time between work and play.

Let us tell you how easy it is to buy a Ford on the Weekly Purchase Plan.

FORD MOTOR COMPANY, DETROIT, MICHIGAN

THE RUNABOUT

# $265

F. O. B. Detroit

Demountable Rims
and Starter $85 extra

THE UNIVERSAL CAR

FORD MOTOR COMPANY
DETROIT, MICH.

Please tell me how I can buy a Ford on small weekly payments.

Name

Address

# Speed up Success!

## What is the man in the picture doing?

*Watching others go by him,* just like thousands of other men, who let the procession of live ones pass them by.

Perhaps he is wondering why these other men of no greater physical strength or mental ability can own automobiles and *ride* towards success while he plods along, year after year, not only not making progress, but actually falling behind.

All of the men whom this by-stander typifies are very like a dormant gasoline engine.

A little cranking of INITIATIVE and a spark of AMBITION would wake them into ACTION, and convert potential power into a reality.

How much you accomplish in the few years when your physical and mental powers can function at highest efficiency depends very largely on the means you employ to SAVE TIME.

If you can move your person twice as fast and apply your personality in twice as many places as some other chap, your chances for success are twice as good as his.

That is where the Chevrolet comes in.

It is more than a time saver; it is a personality multiplier, a time doubler.

If you are one man on your feet you become as two men in a Chevrolet.

Speed up Success! Get there! Keep up with the procession! Enter the great race against Time!

You can do it. There is no intelligent worker so poor he cannot arrange to buy a Chevrolet. There is none so well-off to feel above the grade of this quality car.

Call on the nearest Chevrolet dealer. Find out how easy it is to buy it and how low its operating cost.

### Prices f. o. b. Flint, Michigan

| | |
|---|---|
| Superior Roadster | $490 |
| Superior Touring | 495 |
| Superior Utility Coupe | 640 |
| Superior 4-Passenger Coupe | 725 |
| Superior Sedan | 795 |
| Superior Commercial Chassis | 395 |
| Superior Light Delivery | 495 |
| Utility Express Truck Chassis | 550 |

*Fisher Bodies on all Closed Models*

# Chevrolet Motor Company

*Division of General Motors Corporation*

## Detroit, Mich.

In Canada—Chevrolet Motor Company of Canada, Limited, Oshawa, Ontario

*for Economical Transportation*

*Chevrolet Dealers and Service Stations everywhere. Applications will be considered from high-grade men only, for territory not adequately covered.*

*Five United States manufacturing plants, seven assembly plants and two Canadian plants give us the largest production capacity in the world for high-grade cars and make possible our low prices.*

# The Psychology of the Automobile

The automobile 14,000,000 strong, has in truth become our most numerous "common carrier."

Every owner is in effect a railroad president, operating individually on an elective schedule, over highways built and maintained chiefly at the expense of himself and his fellow motorists.

What has been the effect of the automobile on our composite national mind?—on our social political and economic outlook?

The once poor laborer and mechanic now drives to the building operation or construction job in his own car. He is now a capitalist—the owner of a taxable asset. His wages have been increased from $1.50 or $3.00 a day to $5.00 or $15.00 a day. Before or after acquiring the automobile he has begun paying for a suburban home of his own, and is interested in local improvements, consolidated schools, highways, and community service of various kinds. As a *direct* taxpayer, he votes with care and independence.

Evenings and Sundays he takes his family into the country or to the now near town fifty to one hundred miles away. He has become *somebody*, has a broader and more tolerant view of the one-time cartoon hayseed and the fat-cigared plutocrat.

How can Bolshevism flourish in a motorized country having a standard of living, and thinking too high to permit the existence of an ignorant, narrow, peasant majority?

Is not the automobile entitled to the major credit in this elevation of our standard of citizenship?

## Chevrolet Motor Co. Detroit, Michigan
### *Division of General Motors Corporation*

# MERCEDES

AMERICAN MERCEDES CO., Inc.

Show Rooms Now Located at 247 Park Avenue

Corner 47th Street, New York       Telephone Ashland 7115-7

1925

# PIERCE - ARROW
*Dual-Valve Six*

Series 33—Open Cars $5250, Closed Cars $7000
Series 80 —From $2895 to $4045
at Buffalo, Government Tax Additional

1929

PRINCE OF WALES SEDAN BY FLEETWOOD

# STUTZ SALES CORPORATION
### Ritz Tower, 463 Park Avenue

Telephone Plaza 3275          *Exclusive Agents for Custom Coachwork for Stutz Chasses*

# Somewhere West of Laramie

SOMEWHERE west of Laramie there's a broncho-busting, steer-roping girl who knows what I'm talking about.

She can tell what a sassy pony, that's a cross between greased lightning and the place where it hits, can do with eleven hundred pounds of steel and action when he's going high, wide and handsome.

The truth is—the Playboy was built for her.

Built for the lass whose face is brown with the sun when the day is done of revel and romp and race.

She loves the cross of the wild and the tame.

There's a savor of links about that car—of laughter and lilt and light—a hint of old loves—and saddle and quirt. It's a brawny thing—yet a graceful thing for the sweep o' the Avenue.

Step into the Playboy when the hour grows dull with things gone dead and stale.

Then start for the land of real living with the spirit of the lass who rides, lean and rangy, into the red horizon of a Wyoming twilight.

# JORDAN

JORDAN MOTOR CAR COMPANY, Inc., Cleveland, Ohio

1923

*She drives a Duesenberg*

1932

1934

# 1930 1940

> *We are the first nation in the history
> of the world to go to the poorhouse
> in an automobile.*
>
> —WILL ROGERS

Which car to purchase was a lesser concern to most Americans during the 1930s than finding a job, paying the rent, or buying enough to eat. It seemed as though a vengeful deity, outraged by the florid excesses of the last ten years, had sent a raft of modern plagues to end the fun. The stock market crash, the deepening depression, and then the dust bowl overwhelmed a once optimistic population.

Hundreds of homeless families loaded their belongings onto ancient flivvers and headed West for an imaginary land of milk and honey. They huddled together in "Hoovervilles," slept under "Hoover blankets" (old newspapers), ate "Hoover gravy" (flour and water), and displayed their "Hoover flags" (empty pockets turned inside out).

New heroes replaced Horatio Alger. Dillinger became a modern Robin Hood. And the daredevil exploits of Bonnie and Clyde were turned into a symbol of little people striking back at the heartless banks. The self-portraits Bonnie and Clyde regularly sent to the police always showed them alongside a V-8 Ford.

Henry Ford had intended his new car as something for the masses, and a stimulant to the economy. The government printed posters encouraging the purchase of a car as a step toward prosperity. One car, it was made clear, would provide an auto worker with three months' work. But a new automobile was only a distant dream to the vast majority of Americans in depression America.

Those who couldn't afford a car found other means of escape. Comic book heroes were never so popular. Flash Gordon, Tarzan, and Buck Rogers fought their way to glory in faraway worlds that had never seen a bread line or soup kitchen. As for Little Orphan Annie, well, if things ever got too bad, Daddy Warbucks could always be counted on to straighten them out.

Hollywood offered glittering fantasy worlds as antidotes to reality. If you were broke, you could forget your troubles watching Ginger Rogers (in *Gold Diggers of 1933*), dressed in a bathing suit made of coins, singing "We're in the Money" in Pig Latin. If you couldn't afford to attend the opera or bet at the race track, why not join the Marx Brothers and make a mockery of both? And if you felt just plain lousy, you could let "Little Miss Sunshine," Shirley Temple, into your life. *Nothing* got her down.

Hollywood itself never looked so gay and glamorous as during these bleak, lean years. Gossip columns thrived, as hungry Americans feasted on the exploits of the rich, handsome and carefree royalty of the movies, as well as a new breed of aristocracy, "café society." This was a mélange of old wealth, movie stars, gossip columnists, and publicity hounds, all scrupulously unaffected by the dire economy.

> *However much events of the past few years may have restrained the purchase of fine things, desire for them has been constant. People who, momentarily, feared that they could not afford the best are discovering now that its possession can give confidence, can build morale. . . . from $3200.*
>
> —Lincoln ad, 1934

In a year when the average income was below $1,000, spending $3,200 on a car might be a morale boost indeed! Many who could afford a new car were engaged in the perilous business of securing their position in the now shaky social structure. Naturally, the car one (or one's chauffeur) drove was a crucial indicator of position. Auto ads stressed the equation of social *arrival* to the correct automobile. College students—who were by their very collegiate status well-to-do—appeared in advertisements ruminating about which car they ought to drive upon commencement. In one ad campaign during the 1936 New York Automobile Show, signs appeared in front of "21," Toots Shor's, and all Gotham's swanky clubs: NO PARKING, NOT EVEN BUICKS.

Café society was open to new as well as old wealth, *if* the rules of behavior were obeyed. All one need do to become a Stork Club star was to dress in the latest fashions, affect a slightly zany vivacity, and please the *grande doyenne* of the crowd, a squatty arbiter of the social order from Keokuk, Iowa, named Elsa Maxwell.

For those who needed help in attaining social correctness, there were thick tomes by Margery Wilson and Emily Post on etiquette. These covered everything from how to eat an olive to what to call the manservant. Among Ms. Wilson's suggestions was this advice concerning auto etiquette:

> Ordinarily it is the better part of discretion and good manners not to engage in a lengthy conversation with [one] who is driving a car. . . . If he must talk, let it be more in the nature of a monologue. Any opinion which he may express should be accepted with soothing affirmatives even where the sacrifice of one's dearest principles and strongest convictions are concerned.

Manners were a way of smoothing social intercourse. If a person knew the correct thing to do and say in any situation, one would glide along without friction or effort. However stiff and awkward the rules, their ultimate goal was the streamlining of life.

In some ways the new focus on etiquette was a counterrevolution, restoring what the raucous twenties had undone. Red-hot jazz began to give way to the mellow undulations of swing. Fringed flapper dresses were discarded for curvilinear sweeps of cloth. Modern architecture was long, low, and rounded. And the sporty sedan with the rumble seat faded into the past with the jagged geometry of art deco and the angular movements of the Charleston. Influenced by the Bauhaus, car designers were in pursuit of "the ideal form."

> *Old mother nature has always designed her creatures for the function they are to perform. She has streamlined her fastest fish . . . her swiftest birds . . . her fleetest animals that move on land.*
>
> *You have only to look at a dolphin, a gull, or a greyhound to appreciate the rightness of the tapering, flowing contour of the new Airflow Chrysler.*
>
> *By scientific experiment, Chrysler engineers have simply verified and adapted a natural fundamental law.*
>
> —Chrysler ad, 1934

From locomotive engines (like the Zephyr) to teapots (like Revere Ware), manufactured objects were made to conform to the organic, streamlined shape that symbolized modernity—the teardrop. "A lot of people may not care for the bonnet of the Cord front-drive car," *The New Yorker* reported in 1935. "At first glance it might be a part of a modernistic cottage, or maybe a lamp or refrigerator."

As if to create the quickest way out of the depression quagmire, the car of the 1930s, flanked by blimp and streamlined train, offered an image of effortless movement.

The airplane became a model form. Cars were shown at the airport, parallel to the ultra-modern DC-3. The Aeroform Nash offered the driver "flying power" (1935). Pictured against a background of planets and boomerang curves, enveloped by nebulas of atmospheric gas and veils of intergalactic haze, the impossibly long, low auto of the late thirties seemed ready to sail away to a planet that had never heard of the depression.

By the end of the decade the economy was improving. Having barely acknowledged the depression, auto ads began to look toward a lucrative future. In 1938 General Motors constructed its first "dream car" for public display, the Y-Job. It was a rounded, unbroken form that seemed to represent a culmination of the auto's evolution toward an ideal shape. In 1939 Ford introduced the Lincoln Continental. It was the brainchild of Edsel Ford, Henry's son. The old man wanted nothing to do with this limited-production high-class car. It was a massive streamliner with compound curves and only the sparest decoration. Two years later the Museum of Modern Art proclaimed it a masterpiece of product design.

But the Y-Job and Lincoln Continental were only a glimmer of what the designers had in store. They looked to the future and envisioned whole life-systems in which the automobile played a vital role. The apotheosis of futuristic design came at the World's Fair of 1939 in General Motors' Futurama. Visitors to the mammoth exhibition hall sat in upholstered chairs on a conveyor belt and were whisked along a "magic Aladdin-like flight through time and space." This is what they heard:

> The world, far from being finished, is hardly yet begun. . . . America in 1960 is full of a tanned and vigorous people who in twenty years have learned how to have fun. . . . When Americans of 1960 take their two-month vacations, they drive to the great parklands on giant express highways. A two-way skein consists of four 50-mph lanes on each of the outer edges; two pairs of 75-mph lanes, and in the center, two lanes for 100-mph express traffic. . . . The cars, built like raindrops . . . cost as low as $200.
> Strange? Fantastic? Unbelievable? Remember this is the world of 1960!

The twenty years ahead looked like an unbroken trajectory of progress. There was a war on in Europe, but how could that possibly interrupt the promised perfection of the automobile and the dream life in which it was to play so important a role?

The Ford car has always meant dependable service and honest value. New times have given it further distinction. More and more, with each passing year, it becomes the symbol of progress and the newest, latest developments in automobile building. The Ford goes forward with the needs of the people. • The Ford V-8 reflects that policy. It is thoroughly modern in every detail, with many exclusive improvements and advantages. Ford V-8 means a modern engine in a modern car.

# THE FORD V·8

*In Warner Bros.' "GOLD DIGGERS OF 1935," Buick is featured with Dick Powell and the Berkeley Girls. Warner Bros. consistently choose Buick for shots of lavish musical revue display, and for those depicting people in the modern manner. Today's Buick is exquisitely styled. It harmonizes perfectly with the advanced and newly created styles which Warner Bros. productions display.*

# Hollywood – *Creator of Style* – *Chooses* BUICK *for Its Own*

In brilliant Hollywood—where picture directors and stars create the styles for a nation—Buick plays the star style part. A world once ruled by Paris now looks to Hollywood; and there Buick is the featured car. In production after production, for the hit pictures of the year, Buick is chosen . . . just as it is favored by those who value the prestige of modish, modern design. ¶ All you have ever known or heard of Buick size and roominess . . . of Buick quality and dependability . . . luxury, per-

**$795**
*and up, list prices at Flint.*

formance and economy . . . is now surpassed. To see Buick today is to feast your eyes upon aristocratic, sparkling style. To drive it is to gratify your enthusiasm for unsurpassed performance and to enjoy the unprecedented ease and simplicity of the newest automatic operating features. To ride is to know the finest of all fine motoring. ¶ Twenty-five beautiful models, in four series. Four popular price groups, $795 to $2175, list prices at Flint, Mich. Prices subject to change without notice. Special equipment extra. Favorable G.M.A.C. terms.

BODY BY FISHER . . . A GENERAL MOTORS PRODUCT

## WHEN BETTER AUTOMOBILES ARE BUILT—BUICK WILL BUILD THEM

1935

# IN TUNE

★ ★

• To those who take pride in their homes, their surroundings, their standards of living, a fine motor car is an essential. For thirty-five years Pierce-Arrow has been a symbol of social standing... has fitted naturally into a well-ordered mode of living.

• And so today, with a new spirit in the air, with people everywhere again gratifying their desires for the finer pleasures of life, the supreme comfort and luxury and the distinguished excellence of a Pierce-Arrow are eminently in tune with the times.

*America's Finest Motor Car for America's Finest Families*

THE ENCLOSED DRIVE LIMOUSINE

>>>>> ——————— PIERCE·ARROW ———————→

# "...we'll own a Cadillac, too"

HOW natural it is that young people should think of Cadillac as the finest car to own. In Washington, they have seen Cadillac cars before the doors of diplomats and statesmen . . . in New York, at the entrances of the most exclusive clubs . . . in San Francisco, on fashionable Nob Hill. Throughout all America youth has literally grown up in the knowledge that Cadillac stands for the ultimate in personal transportation. . . . Perhaps you are one who, not so long ago, planned sometime to enjoy the unusual performance and comfort of a distinguished Cadillac car. If so, your goal is at hand. For Cadillac cars today are the finest in every way that Cadillac has ever built, yet they are offered at the lowest prices in many years. Your Cadillac dealer will gladly give you price details and information on the convenient G.M.A.C. payment plan. Why not go to him for an appraisal of your present car, and a delightful demonstration of a new Cadillac?

1935

# Whenthree's *not* a crowd

When there's an important selling job to be done, after hours, on some moonlit roadway, or shadowy campus drive, nothing gets you off to a better start than one of those new sport roadsters being built by Chevrolet.

The front seat has plenty of room for the great American blonde, *yourself*, and several tons of raccoon coat—as well as a second blonde, if you believe in numbers. Then, if some offensive male decides that he'll go along too, there's a pleasantly remote rumble seat, where he can be placed in cold storage indefinitely.

In addition—with Syncro-Mesh and Free Wheeling, you can let the car practically drive itself. Chevrolet's six-cylinder motor runs so noiselessly that you can put across your personality without using a gold-lined megaphone.

And just as the Chevrolet Six never cramps your technique, it never cramps the allowance, either. Gas, oil, and servicings can be paid for, with plenty of change left over for cover charges and refreshments. And as for first-cost—well, bless your soul—just snap on the bifocals and take a look to the right!

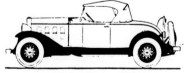

*The Sport Roadster, $495*

*Twenty beautiful new models, at prices ranging from* **$475 to $660**

All prices f. o. b. Flint, Mich., special equipment extra. Low delivered prices and easy G. M. A. C. terms. Chevrolet Motor Company, Detroit, Michigan. Division of General Motors.

## NEW CHEVROLET SIX

*The Great American Value for 1932*

1935

1935

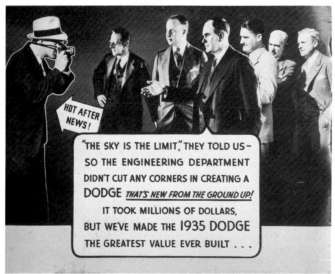

LUXURY LINER DE LUXE *Seven Passenger Limousine*

## "HERE COME THE HOYTS"

THERE is something about a Pierce-Arrow that
brings a friendly wave of the hand from traffic-
officers...Even truckmen pull over a little more
quickly, and doormen salute a little more smartly.

This instinctive deference is not due to the distinctive appearance of the car . . . nor its extra-
ordinary comfort . . . nor the unparalleled control
of its full-power brakes . . . nor even the quiet
smoothness of its engine, so superb that it recently
broke 14 world records for speed and endurance.

No one feature is responsible. The only expla-
nation is that Pierce-Arrows are Pierce-Arrows.
And the new models of 1934 will tend to deserve
and to extend this deference.

PIERCE ARROW

1934

# "...and the dear man thought he sold me!"

The Hat... Erik's black felt pill box from Bergdorf Goodman

The Jacket... Yvonne Carette designed it herself ...it's short and chunky in black fox

The Car... a Chrysler Royal Touring Sedan

"OF COURSE, John is a lamb . . . but he has to be handled.

"So when he began assembling Chrysler catalogs, I just said, 'Certainly, a home in Newport would be nice, too!'

"And he began to tell me all about Chrysler invading the low-priced field—as if I'd never heard it! Although when I *saw* the 1938 Chrysler Royal, I didn't quite see how such a car could be low-priced!

"Well, we rode in one. And while John kept prattling about horsepower and valves and gasoline mileage, I drank in the beauty and quality . . . the size . . . the room . . . the gorgeous instrument panel . . . the marvelous upholstery.

"I think we both made up our minds when we got to the railroad tracks on Sixth Street. We braced ourselves as usual . . . but that love of a Chrysler just glided over them as if they weren't there at all.

"So John took up weight distribution, and hydraulic shock absorbers and independently sprung front wheels . . . and I just asked him gently if Chrysler engineering wasn't reputed to be the best in the industry. He said it was. So I told him we could probably accept what everybody knew.

"Really, we were both amazed at the low price . . . and the order signing was brisk and pleasant.

"At dinner, John explained the hypoid rear axle . . . and I let him. The dear man had it coming . . . he thought *he* had sold *me!*"

\* \* \*

☆ **NEW 1938 ROYAL** . . . 95 horsepower, 119-inch wheelbase. Ten body types.
☆ **NEW 1938 IMPERIAL** . . . 110 horsepower, 125-inch wheelbase. Six body types.
☆ **NEW 1938 CUSTOM IMPERIAL** . . . 130 horsepower, 144-inch wheelbase. Three body types.
**Tune in on Major Bowes, Columbia Network, every Thursday, 9 to 10:00 P. M., Eastern Standard Time.**

**ROYAL** . . . MORE FOR THE MONEY IN THE LOW-PRICED FIELD!

**IMPERIAL** . . . PHENOMENAL PERFORMANCE AT A REMARKABLE PRICE!

# Chrysler
## BETTER Engineered... BETTER Made!

# *A New Era of Transportation*
# BRINGS FUNCTIONAL DESIGN

*New era in railroad transportation—Streamlined passenger train*

*Automobile streamlining on the continent as featured at recent Berlin Auto Show*

A new era of transportation has arrived—an era whose influence is revolutionizing transportation in every field, changing all precedent and obsoleting all the hide-bound traditions inherited from a horse-and-buggy age. It is an era that is fashioning all modes of transportation to a better performance of their functions. ☆ Exhaustive research has demonstrated the tremendous inefficiency and extravagant waste of power of conventionally shaped vehicles in battling wind resistance. Just put your hand out of a car window going at 30 miles per hour—then do the same at 60. Notice the tremendous difference in air pressure on your hand. From this simple test some idea is gained of the resistance encountered in propelling the conventional car over the highways. At 50 miles per hour the conventional car of the old horse-and-buggy design will waste approximately half its fuel overcoming wind resistance. ☆ When nature forms her creatures for speed, she shapes them in smooth lines from a rounded head to a tapering tail in order to overcome the resistance of their environment, whether it be air or water. ☆ Chrysler engineers have departed from the conventional and have designed the new Airflow Chrysler in accordance with this basic natural law. In these daring new models the lines of the gracefully rounded front end sweep smoothly over the flowing curves of the body to the sloping, tapering rear. ☆ All of the air disturbing appendages, fenders, head lamps, horns—have been covered and the new Airflow Chrysler slips through the air so perfectly that wind roar, present in conventional cars at high speed, is eliminated.

*Ultra modern transportation and architecture—Graf Zeppelin over Chrysler Building*

# *—and CHRYSLER brings*
# FLOATING RIDE

1934

"And when the boy grows older – he'll be just as comfortable and safe in a
*KNEE-ACTION CHEVROLET!*"

*We'll* venture to say that this boy won't permit himself to become very much older without clamoring for his first ride in that wonderful new Chevrolet!

And his parents are right! He *will* be every bit as comfortable in a Knee-Action Chevrolet* as he is in his bed at home. For Knee-Action steps over little "ripples" in the road, as well as big bumps, and gives the smoothest ride known, as millions of Knee-Action users will tell you.

And he'll be *safe*, too! For Knee-Action levels out the ride, keeps the car perfectly steady on any road and at any speed, gives the driver *better steering* and *better control* than he could possibly have without it.

You're missing a lot if you aren't enjoying the many advantages of Chevrolet's Knee-Action Gliding Ride. It's so safe, so comfortable, so different! Better visit your nearest Chevrolet dealer today and order the only low-priced car that has Knee-Action*—the new 1937 Chevrolet!

CHEVROLET MOTOR DIVISION, *General Motors Sales Corporation*, DETROIT, MICHIGAN

*Knee-Action and Shockproof Steering on Master De Luxe models only. General Motors Installment Plan— monthly payments to suit your purse.

**CHEVROLET**

*The Complete Car – Completely New*

1937

1940

*B*ENEATH THE OUTWARD BEAUTY of the Lincoln-Zephyr, in closed types, is the famous unit-body-and-frame. Consisting of a framework of steel trusses welded into a single structure, the construction affords great protective strength and rigidity. With both front and rear seats near the center, car weight is well distributed. This balance is an important factor in the exceptionally fine ride received by both front and rear seat passengers. The large glass area and narrow pillars also contribute to rider enjoyment.

1940

# BIG, RUGGED, DEPENDABLE
## THE NEW 1940 DODGE IS A MODEL OF MODERN SAFETY

**SUPER-TOUGH AMOLA** steel in springs, gears, axles and 19 other vital points gives an extra margin of safety and dependability that affords not only priceless protection, but adds thousands of miles to the life of these important parts. Amola Steel, you know, is one of the metallurgical marvels of the age! It is tougher, stronger—amazingly resistant to wear and tear!

A RED BLOODED CAR IF THERE EVER WAS ONE!

**ROARING AT TOP SPEED** . . . Jimmie Lynch about to put his Dodge car through one of the most fiendish tests man ever devised! Day after day, this daredevil driver subjects his Dodge cars to almost unbelievable punishment!

**JIMMIE LYNCH**, the man who makes a living laughing at death! He and his "Death Dodgers" risk their life every day at the New York World's Fair putting Dodge cars through death-defying stunts no ordinary car could survive!

**THERE HE GOES!** . . . Leaping through thin air, Death Dodger Jimmie Lynch depends on the in-built safety and ruggedness of Dodge cars to bring him safely through this spectacular demonstration of skill and daring!

**BACK TO EARTH AGAIN!** "Only Dodge could take the beating I give a car every day!" says Jimmie. "Dodge has saved my life literally hundreds of times! I'd be a sucker to use any other car!"

## "The Greatest Brakes I Know Of!"

*Self-Energizing Hydraulic Brakes*

*Dodge Equal-Pressure Hydraulic Brakes*

**Says JIMMIE LYNCH Famed Daredevil Driver**

"In my work, I not only have to have a car that is dependable and can stand the gaff, but that car has to have brakes that I know I can depend on," says Mr. Lynch. "I know them all, and I know that no other brakes can equal Dodge hydraulic brakes. You know that Dodge pioneered in the development of hydraulic brakes, and this valuable experience that can be gained only through time is reflected in the Dodge brakes of today — the greatest brakes I know of!"

**IT'S PEDAL FEEL THAT COUNTS!** Dodge equal-pressure hydraulic brakes do not have the "wrapping action" peculiar to self-energizing brakes. They give you the right "pedal feel" because you don't have to "jam" them on to get the desired response. Braking pressure at the wheel is always in direct ratio to foot pressure at the pedal. You *always* get smooth, sure stops!

**F**LASHING along the highway, the new 1940 Dodge captures the gaze of all with its thrilling new beauty and dashing style. But remember this—to protect you and your family, this year's Dodge brings an even greater measure of safety than ever before!

In one important way after another the new 1940 Luxury Liner gives you the protection you need! Hair-trigger power to whisk you out of danger spots! Famous Dodge hydraulic brakes that you can *always* count on! All-steel body, with steel walls, steel floor, steel roof! These are only a few of the ways Dodge protects you and yours! Read about the many more safety advantages pictured here!

**INGENIOUS** safety door lock located on the door moulding. You press the button to lock the door. Lock can be released only by lifting button. A safety feature of vital importance to parents of small children!

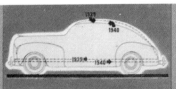

**BUILT CLOSER TO THE GROUND!** The dotted line shows how the over-all height of the new 1940 Dodge has been reduced to bring a still lower center of gravity and add to the roadability and safety of this year's Dodge. Although the roof has been lowered, headroom is the same!

**INSTRUMENT PANEL** is smooth and fin. Back of front seat is heavily tufted to p[ro]tect rear seat passengers in case of emergency stop. Door handles are smoo[th] rounded and curve inward for safety!

The Coupe

The Twelve (Model 1240)
175 Horsepower . . .
139-inch Wheelbase

The Eight (Model 840)
140 Horsepower . . .
139-inch Wheelbase

# "LIKE A BAT OUT OF HELL!"

## THE JEEP FROM WILLYS-OVERLAND

THROUGH clouds of flying sand and gravel it is roaring across the panorama of today's war, "like a bat out of hell"—the JEEP from Willys-Overland.

Tough soldiers idolize this modern mustang of metal—which gives them power, speed, action, reliability—and a seemingly *bottomless* gas tank.

And *we* are proud of Willys-Overland civilian engineers, who collaborated with expert engineers of

the U. S. Quartermaster Corps to produce the Jeep.

These are the same fine engineers who created the Willys Go-Devil Engine and the Willys Americar—the war-time engineering aces of whom it is now said—"they get more *power, speed, action* and *durability* out of a ton of steel and a gallon of gasoline than has ever been done before."

Here again, and most strikingly, the fundamental soundness and versatility of Willys engineering and

production practice, plus extensive facilities and broad experience, are proving out in the most relentless testing laboratory of all—the laboratory of war.

*This is an all-out war for everybody. Do your part. Conserve rubber, tin and other vital materials. Buy war bonds and stamps. Pay taxes with a smile. Democracy is fighting for its life. Whatever the total price you pay it will be as nothing compared to the priceless value of continued Freedom. Willys-Overland Motors, Inc.*

U. S. ARMY JEEP

# WILLYS

### MOTOR CARS    TRUCKS AND JEEPS

AMERICAR
the People's Car

THE GO-DEVIL ENGINE—power-heart of WILLYS CARS and all JEEPS

1940    1950

*This is the last V-8. Watch out Japs.*
*Here come the little jeeps next.*
*V for VICTORY.*

—WORKERS' SIGN ON THE LAST FORD OFF THE
ASSEMBLY LINE, FEBRUARY 10, 1942

The promise of the 1939 Futurama was about to be broken. The coming of war at first appeared to be merely an interruption in the country's steady climb out of the depression toward prosperity. After Pearl Harbor, it was time to roll up our sleeves and quickly lick the tar out of the enemy. Early in 1942 automobile production ceased and car manufacturers retooled for the war.

What happened was nothing short of a miracle. In 1940 the U.S. Army had ranked seventeenth in strength among all armies of the world. Industry applied something that became known as American know-how and soon produced the most efficient armed force in the world.

No aspect of life on the home front was untouched. Women turned in their nylon stockings to be made over into gunpowder bags. Instead of wearing nylons, they painted "seams" on their legs with eyebrow pencils. Bacon grease and cooking fat were turned into explosives. A single rubber tire could be made into twelve gas masks. Those who had cars learned to baby them. They learned not to brake too hard, lest precious rubber be left on the pavement. Americans learned to repair, tune, and service their cars; and during the course of all this effort to prolong automobiles' lives, it became obvious how important the car had become. Hardest of all was learning to live on a gas ration allotment of three gallons per week.

Shortly before the war auto ads began to appear that were somewhat ominous and darkly shaded. Graceful design gave way to raw power.

Then, as the fighting began, all stops were pulled. Like Hollywood's films about the war, ads hammered home their message. Auto makers showed, in dramatic perspective, tight close-ups, and violent colors, what they were doing to beat hell out of the enemy. The message rang out loud—Detroit was getting the job done.

Toward the end of the war, ads grew softer in hue, even nostalgic. They began to talk of home and the good old days—and the role of the automobile in the American way of life.

By 1945, with the end of the war at hand, it seemed certain that when the same know-how that won the war was applied to the postwar car, it would create wondrous vehicles for private use. It was fully expected after the wartime success of American air power that the car of the future would incorporate the most spectacular advances in airborne technology. Sure enough, in 1948 fins appeared on the Cadillac (inspired by the P-38 fighter). It was not, however, until the 1950s that the copywriter's prose began to suggest that autos, complete with fins, "rocket" engines, and "triple turbine takeoff," could really fly.

The future looked good. The American work force was fully mobilized and ready to produce the consumer's paradise that had been deferred. Dozens of "all-new" cars were suddenly announced by would-be auto makers who wanted to get the postwar jump on Detroit. They ranged from a three-wheel 500-pound bump-em car called the Davis to a sports car sold by Madman Muntz, the California used-car salesman.

The most controversial and most nearly successful of the dream cars was the Tucker. It was designed to cruise at 100 mph and was equipped with safety features that were twenty-five years ahead of their time. It was a revolutionary car. Preston Tucker showed it around the country, raising $25 million to go into production. But by mid-1948, rumors spread that the car was a swindle. Tucker was attacked by news commentator Drew Pearson, then indicted by the government for fraud. He was acquitted, but the scandal killed the car. A few of the fifty Tuckers built are still around today. Some remember Preston Tucker as the consummate con man; others as a visionary genius, shot down for his radical originality.

But even if the tantalizing predictions of postwar wondermobiles couldn't be realized, any car was, in Buick's words, "So nice to come home to." After four years of bouncing on a jeep at the front or nursing a tired jalopy at home, Americans were ready to indulge themselves.

In 1946, 714 million gallons of ice cream were eaten. America was hungry for all that it had missed. *House Beautiful* said that it was time for GI Jane to "retool with ruffles." The wartime look, with its drab, spartan fashions "inspired" by military garb, gave way to Christian Dior's New Look from Paris. The slacks, goggles, and machinist's gloves that Rosie the Riveter had worn to win the war were traded in for flowered dresses, lacy veils, and white gloves. Uniforms were replaced by extravagant double-breasted suits. The strapless bra was invented in 1946, the Toni home permanent in 1947.

Fashion replaced form. Auto ads no longer spoke of "nature's laws" but of the latest look. Fredrica, "designer for members of the Imperial Hungarian Court," appeared in Kaiser-Frazer ads to praise the car's "rich and harmonious use of colors and fabrics" (1948). Claire McCardell of Townley Frocks, Inc., studied the Kaiser-Frazer and concluded: "No wonder women fall in love with them" (1949). Buick proclaimed itself "Fashion Plate for '48."

It was during the late 1940s that automatic transmission was first widely offered on American automobiles. This technological step was as important to the future of motoring as the self-starter had been during the teens. One Buick ad described it as providing a "freedom that was unknown four years ago . . . freedom from physical strain . . . freedom from tension . . . a new mastery of time, distance, straightaway, curve, upgrade and the open road." What it provided, really, was the freedom to drive without any mechanical thought. More than ever, driving could be just second nature.

Cars were ever more comfortable, too. They began to resemble the very place that GIs had longed for—the home. Ford called its 1949 model "a living room on wheels," with "sofa seats" and "picture-window visibility" (Ford brochure, 1949). The Airflyte Nash, introduced in 1949, featured fold-down seats, and thus became in effect a "bedroom on wheels."

Such comfort spelled trouble to some. Combined with the sheer exuberance of limitless driving (in part, a reaction to gas rationing), the car's convenience for youthful indiscretions was the source of alarm in books such as *Teen-Age Vice* by Courtney Ryley Cooper. During the forties, with most men over eighteen in the army, there was a new focus of attention on what was first called "the teenager." Cooper's book, which purported to be "inspired" by J. Edgar Hoover, went through six printings at the beginning of the decade. He warned:

> Today's highways are a shuttle of the outpouring of beauty shops, the spew of race tracks and gambling joints, and traveling hordes of jitterbugs, "pig-joint" or barbecue girls, "jook girls" from the southern points, . . . college town prostitutes [and] thousands of professional young hitchhikers of both sexes, out to fulfill their desire to see what is on the other side of the fence.

Whatever the car's contributions to "teen-age vice," Cooper's inflammatory prose could hardly be said to speak for any more than a tiny minority of forties youth. It was a clean-cut generation; its heroes (according to *Life* magazine) included Doris Day, Roy Rogers, and Florence Nightingale. And if they did get a little giddy when Frank Sinatra, the King of Swoon, appeared, that was really nothing to worry about.

It was during the 1940s that the teenager staked his claim on the automobile. The "hot rod" was in part spawned by the dearth of cars during the war. It was assembled from pieces of old cars—a V-8 engine, a Model A body, and no muffler. Hot rods, jalopies, and drive-in movies were as much a part of the teenager's life as the slumber party, the jukebox, and baggy rolled-up jeans. Between 1947 and 1950, two thousand new drive-in movie theaters were built in America.

New faces were seen in millions of American homes: Milton Berle, Hopalong Cassidy, Gertrude Berg, and Howdy Doody. Like those television personalities, the automobile was becoming a part of family life. Indeed, cars began to evolve distinct personalities during the postwar years. No doubt about it—they even grew faces.

In Europe they called the 1950 Buick's terrible, toothy grille the "dollar grin." The '50 Oldsmobile had a more dour look, with downturned chrome grille and tear-shaped directional signal pods. The Cadillac began to sport a rich smile. The Packard still had the pursed lips of patrician nobility.

But these cars were more than just a pretty face. Their bodies were long, low, and heavy. They exuded confidence, a sense of unswervable purpose. They were substantial-looking, and seemed to symbolize an irrevocable forward motion.

Some looked like friends, others like warrior allies. The station wagon, a car at this time for use around one's estate for menial tasks, was undeniably snobby, the way only a servant of the very rich can be. Its wood body had to be varnished yearly, and its delicate skin required an indoor garage. It was the convertible that seemed to epitomize what the auto had become. It was freedom, the open road, wind-in-your-face, carefree driving.

But there was work to be done, too. The sense of purpose implicit in automobile design suggests the crucial role cars were going to play in creating the good life promised by the postwar years. And so millions of Americans, newly in love with the auto, or with an old friendship rekindled, moved out to the suburbs, where thirty million war babies were about to grow up.

55

1942

# GENERAL MOTORS?
## *RIGHT HERE ON MAIN STREET*

Of course you will find dealers who sell General Motors cars in your home town—you probably know one or more of them.

But—what is equally important—you will find them on every Main Street from coast to coast and from border to border.

In the course of providing their own customers with the service of trained mechanics and with quality parts, they make it possible for every man or woman who owns a General Motors car to find prompt and reliable service on thousands of Main Streets throughout America.

These dealers are our partners in progress. Our job is to furnish them with the finest motor-car values that GM research can develop or GM manufacturing resources can produce. Their job is to bring these cars to market—and keep them rolling through years of use.

They bring to that job a steadily increasing skill in management, a standard of business judgment that entitles them to recognition as one of the finest groups of merchants in America. They are just that, with mighty few exceptions.

And they are something more. They are valuable assets to any community — good men to know as neighbors and friends.

GENERAL MOTORS · GENERAL MOTORS DEALERS

*Partners in* **PROGRESS** *through* **SERVICE**

**GENERAL MOTORS**

CHEVROLET · PONTIAC · OLDSMOBILE
BUICK · CADILLAC

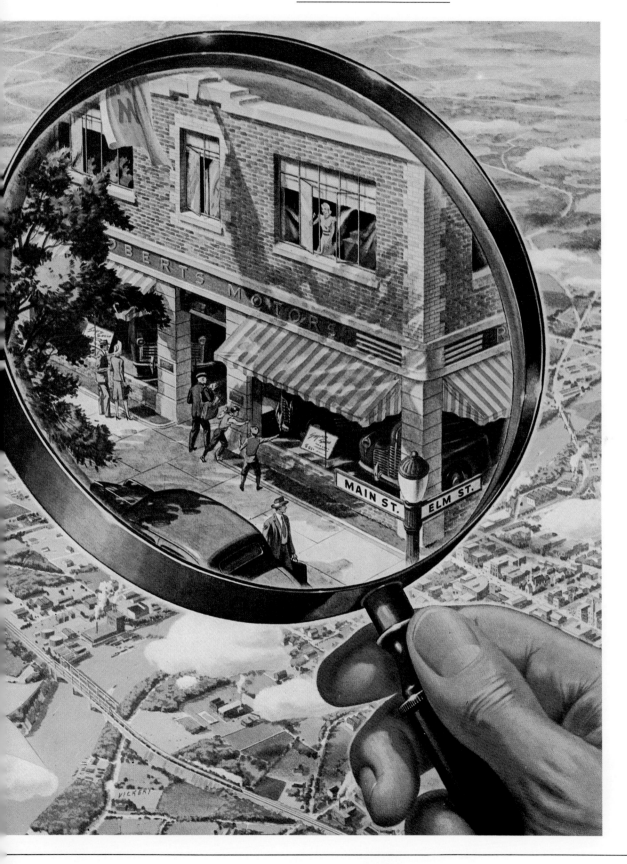

1941

# Making its mark.. on a Nazi Mark IV

OUTMANEUVERED at every turn by the harrying tactics of a squadron of high speed American M-5 light tanks, this formidable Nazi Mark IV tank has been immobilized by a well placed hit in its vital mechanism.

The M-5 has been in production at the Cadillac Motor Car Division for over a year. But so perfectly was this military secret kept that few outside Cadillac plants knew of its existence before it swept into battle.

Army Ordnance engineers, familiar with every phase of tank operation, joined forces with Cadillac engineers in developing the M-5. As a result, the M-5 incorporates all that is latest and best in light tank practice plus two innovations from Cadillac peacetime engineering. This accounts for its high speed and great maneuverability.

Likewise entrusted to us are more than 170 vital parts manufactured to extremely close tolerances for America's foremost liquid-cooled aircraft engine. These and other assignments on which Cadillac craftsmen are engaged to the fullest production capacity in our history are war production jobs which take full advantage of all that the Cadillac reputation and tradition imply.

CADILLAC MOTOR CAR DIVISION  GENERAL MOTORS CORPORATION

1943

# I WANT <u>UP</u>!

It's dark down here.

It's quiet down here.

It's lonely down here.

No light. Just the glow of emergency bulbs. No noise. Just the ebb and flow of air in our lungs. No talking. But a lot of thinking.

We're "on the bottom."

They're waiting for us up there. They're listening for us up there. For the turn of a screw, for the clang of a wrench on the deck to tell their next depth bomb where to go.

We're waiting, too. For the sound of their engines to die away or—for the gagging stink of chlorine gas that lets us know our hull is cracked, the batteries are flooded and we're going down in a bubble of air and oil to drown!

Somehow, sweating it out down here in the cold and the dark and the fear, it seems to me I get things straighter than I used to. I see things clear.

I know now what this war's about. I know what this war is being fought for. I want this war over quick—and when it's over, I want up!

That's what I'm fighting for—*up!*

For the right to stand up in the world with my bride by my side and her hand on my arm.

For the right to speak up in my town and have my say and then sit down.

For the right every night to run up the steps of my house back home and pick up and hold a son of my own.

For his right and her right and mine to grow up, to work up in the same America I left behind . . . where there's freedom to breathe . . . freedom to move up to new and better things . . . to look up to the skies and recognize that in America there will always be a limitless opportunity to rise as high, to go as far as courage and strength and ability can take me!

That's how I remember America.

Keep it that way . . . until I come back.

· · · ·

*Here at Nash-Kelvinator, we're building 2,000 h. p. Pratt & Whitney engines for Navy Vought Corsair fighters . . . making intricate Hamilton Standard propellers . . . readying production lines to build Sikorsky helicopters for the Army Air Forces . . . doing our part to keep for our boys while they're away the same America they've always known . . . a land of progress and enterprise and equality for all.*

· · · ·

NASH-KELVINATOR CORPORATION
*Kenosha · Milwaukee · DETROIT · Grand Rapids · Lansing*

NASH
AUTOMOBILES
KELVINATOR
REFRIGERATORS · ELECTRIC RANGES

ENLIST NOW! BACK THE ATTACK — WITH WAR BONDS. **THIRD WAR LOAN DRIVE.**

YOU'LL BE "ON THE BEAM" . . .

## There's a *Ford* in your future!

It's a picture that will have to wait. America has an important job to do before your smart, peacetime Ford can be produced.

. . . But when your new Ford does arrive, you'll be proud of it. For it will be big and roomy—have plenty of "go". Its styling will be youthful, beautiful.

Inside and out, it will be rich appearing —with many refinements. Naturally, it will be thrifty and reliable—as all Ford cars have been for more than 40 years. . . . Yes, exciting new fun is in the offing for you. For some day the necessary word will come through. And we'll be ready to start our production plans. Un-

til that time, however, the full Ford resources will continue to be devoted to the needs of final Victory.

*FORD MOTOR COMPANY*

"THE FORD SHOW". Brilliant singing stars, orchestra and chorus. Every Sunday, NBC network. 2:00 P.M., E.W.T., 1:00 P.M., C.W.T., 12:00 M., M.W.T., 11:00 A.M., P.W.T.

BUY MORE WAR BONDS

BUY STILL MORE WAR BONDS

This is the 1942 Buick which sets the high standards to be surpassed in new models now being made ready.

WHEN BETTER AUTOMOBILES ARE BUILT

BUICK WILL BUILD THEM

1945

**THE DRIVE THAT WAS PROVED IN ARMY TANKS**
Since its introduction in the 1940 Oldsmobile, Hydra-Matic Drive has been thoroughly owner-proved in billions of miles of driving. And it was thoroughly *battle-proved*, during the war, in thousands of Army tanks. In the application of this automatic drive to Army vehicles, important advancements were made in smoothness and reliability, which are incorporated in the new and finer Hydra-Matic Drive offered in the 1946 Oldsmobile.

1946

_Fredrica_

## OBSERVES "MAJOR INNOVATIONS" IN THE KAISER AND THE FRAZER

Fredrica is the designer-name chosen by the fourth generation of illustrious couturiers—a family once famed as designers for members of the Imperial Hungarian Court. Today Fredrica stands out as designer and producer of furs for the world's most discriminating clientele.

Fredrica says about the KAISER and the FRAZER, "a rich and harmonious use of colors and fabrics unique in the field of transportation— major innovations that add new zest and pleasure to motor car ownership."

Fredrica joins more than a dozen of the world's foremost designers in acclaiming the truly functional design and exclusive style features of the KAISER and the FRAZER.

**KAISER-FRAZER CORPORATION • WILLOW RUN, MICHIGAN**

_Full-length fitted Safari Alaska Sealskin, featuring removable short cape. Hat by John Frederics_

## KAISER

## FRAZER

1948

# The First Completely

**PRESTON TUCKER**

President, Tucker Corporation. One of the nation's top designers and builders of special cars and inventor of many of the improvements in automotive design owned by Tucker Corporation—patents on which have either been issued or are pending.

## The Facts About Tucker Financing and the Tucker Plant

THE WORLDWIDE response to the recent Tucker stock offering is proof of the confidence the public has in the Tucker Corporation policies. The completion of this financing program now gives the Tucker Corporation ample working capital from the sale of stock and from dealer franchise sales.

As a result, the War Assets Administration has now given Tucker Corporation a long-term lease on the great former B-29 engine plant in Chicago with option to buy.

This plant—now the *Tucker Plant*—is the largest, most modern automotive plant in the world. It is ideally suited for making a com-

pletely new car. It was laid out by automotive men for the most economical volume production, built by the Government and equipped with the newest, finest, automatic machines for volume production.

Only a manufacturer starting fresh in a plant like this could build the Tucker '48. Only an executive with Preston Tucker's background and determination to build such a car could lead so many top automotive men to pool patents, talents and resources in a common cause.

Already production lines to turn out a thousand cars a day are being set up in this plant.

## The Success Story of the Year

YES, millions are already thrilling to the news of a *completely new* car. Not the conventional design with a few annual model changes such as you are being asked to accept as new this year, as in past years. Not just new-*looking*, but new in driving performance, too, with dozens of exciting engineering features never before seen in a volume production car.

### TESTED ON THE SPEEDWAY

How Preston Tucker developed these new features in fifteen years of rigid tests is a story of rare vision and courage. During these years he was a partner of the late Harry Miller in building the famous Miller Special cars which won 11 out of 15 annual Speedway Classics at Indianapolis.

In these years Preston Tucker created designs so advanced that even now no conventional automotive plant could produce them in volume without scrapping tools worth millions.

Later, when war came, Preston Tucker went to Washington and developed engineering features for motorized vehicles and aircraft. These and all other war materials were needed in such quantities that the Government spared no expense to create new plants and new mass production techniques.

This is why Preston Tucker today can start from scratch in the largest and most modern plant in the world . . . why he can build a car at a medium price with engineering features which up to now have only been built expensively by hand.

### ALL ATTENDANCE RECORDS BROKEN

More than a million and a half motorists have already thrilled to the sight of this exciting new car. In special showings in New York, Chicago, Toronto, St. Louis, Milwaukee, Boston, Philadelphia, Los Angeles, and Washington it has broken all attendance records.

When you see it, you will realize how fortunate you are if you're in the market for a new car. For before many months you can own the first completely new car in half a century . . . a car in the medium- not the high-priced field, yet years ahead in performance, comfort, and in safety, too.

**Fred Rockelman,** Executive Vice President, Director of Sales. Formerly President Plymouth Division of Chrysler Corp. and General Sales Manager Ford Motor Co.

### These men are the builders of the Tucker '48

Preston Tucker heads a group of executives who are honored names in the automotive industry. Each has left his imprint on the methods of manufacture and distribution of motor cars in use today.

Now these men are making automotive history all over again, building a car that will be the inspiration of engineers for years to come.

**Lee S. Treese,** Vice President, Charge of Manufacturing. Formerly Production Executive of Ford Motor Co.

**K. E. Lyman,** Tech. Ass to the President. Engineeri consultant with long Bo Warner and Bendix experien

OF TESTING PRODUCED

# New Car in Fifty Years

*128-inch wheel base.*
*Yet only 5 feet high from road to roof.*
*150-horsepower rear engine.*

*You'll Step Into a New Automotive Age when You Drive Your*

# Tucker '48

## The Amazing SAFETY FEATURES of This Car Will Set a FUTURE PATTERN for the Industry

**Entirely New Safety Features.** Conventional instrument panel replaced by attractive sponge rubber crash-board cowl, under which is spacious safety chamber protected by steel bulkheads. Front seat occupants can drop into this space in a split second in case of unavoidable collision... The center "Cyclops Eye," located between special focussed-beam headlights, turns with the wheels to light way around curves and corners ... Rear-engine design has lower center of gravity than any other mass production car, making it virtually impossible to overturn.

**Rear Engine.** 150-horsepower, flat opposed 6-cylinder engine located below level of passengers. More power for weight of car than any automotive engine ever built.

Prevents fumes, heat and noise from flowing back through the passenger compartment.

**Electronic High Frequency Ignition** delivers a hotter, more lasting spark. Gas in the cylinder is completely consumed, thus doing away with engine knocks. Assures all-weather push-button speed in starting.

**Precision Balance.** The unique Tucker design distributes weight to give maximum safety, maximum power transmission, hairline steering and driving control, and — for the first time — complete four-wheel traction in braking. Only a rear engine can achieve precision balance — for years the goal of automotive engineers.

**Single Disc Brakes.** There are no conventional brake

bands to wear, no periodic adjustments. These new-type, air-cooled hydraulic brakes are 63% more effective, have 2½ times more braking surface than conventional brakes. Insure straight-line stopping (even on ice) without jostling passengers. The same type brakes that stop fast-landing military planes without skid or turn.

**Individual Wheel Suspension.** The new Tucker individual wheel suspension cushions each wheel by its own rubber torsional action arm, actually erasing shock instead of simply softening it. This unique suspension system also eliminates gyroscopic forces, thus preventing the Tucker '48 from veering with the wind and weaving or pitching at touring speeds.

**W. Dulian,** Sales Manager. Formerly Sales Executive Buick Div. of General Motors, with long experience Dodge and Studebaker.

**Herbert Morley,** Vice President and Director of Procurement. Formerly Plant Manager Detroit manufacturing units of Norge Division, Borg Warner Corporation.

**Ben Parsons,** Vice President, Chief Engineer. Former consultant and internationally known authority on simplification and fuel injection.

## *A Completely New Car –*
## Yet with Engineering Principles
## Completely Proved

*Address All Inquiries to*
TUCKER CORPORATION, 7401 South Cicero Ave., Chicago 29, Illinois
*Send export inquiries to Tucker Export Corp., 39 Pearl St., New York 4, N. Y.*

1947

1954

# 1950    1960

*Today the American Road has no end; the road that went nowhere now goes everywhere. . . . The wheels move on endlessly, always moving, always forward—and always lengthening the American Road. On that road the nation is steadily traveling beyond the troubles of this century, constantly heading toward finer tomorrows. The American Road is paved with hope.*

—FORD AD, 1951

Travel had once been a luxury reserved mostly for the rich or rootless. No more. Once a week throughout the 1950s the American public tuned in to Dinah Shore's serenade: "See the U.S.A. in Your Chevrolet." The decade began with a promise of the good life. The "futuramic" dream pinched back by war was ready to flower.

The good life meant mobility. Car culture was booming. In 1951 Charles Kemmons Wilson, a real estate developer, had a bright idea—the franchised motel. It was to be clean, secure and inviting—all the things that sleazy roadside motor courts were not. It was to be a place you could take your family instead of your mistress. And it was to be the same from coast to coast. It was called the Holiday Inn.

The first McDonald's opened in 1955. Like the Holiday Inn, it offered "no surprises." It was clean, fast, convenient, and—for a nation in love with the auto—it was fun. What better place to eat a burger than in your Bel-Air convertible?

In 1956 ground was broken for the interstate highway system—forty thousand miles of unlimited American horizons, not to mention the construction jobs and roadside enterprise that were prophesied along the way. The interstate was made possible by the Highway Trust Fund, a multibillion-dollar account made up of car and gasoline taxes that enabled the federal government to pick up 90 percent of the tab for highway construction.

"What's good for the country is good for General Motors." When Charles E. Wilson, president of General Motors, made that statement in 1953, it was both an observation and a prediction. Cars were good for America. In 1955 President Eisenhower said, "Automobiles mean progress for our country, greater happiness, and greater standards of living." There seemed to be no limit to the role the automobile was destined to play.

However motoramically mobile the postwar life promised to be, it all began at home. In Levittown or Los Angeles the two-car garage became an integral part of split-level architecture. A new car was a sure way to keep up with the Joneses.

As suburbs grew, public transportation disintegrated. Suburbanites were in the business of raising families (all those war babies!). The car was an essential tool:

> *Darling! That's the car for me. It's as easy to handle as a baby carriage. And it's so roomy. There's enough seating space for Tommy's Cub Scout den. Plenty of cargo space for all those odd-shaped packages I acquire during the day, too.*
> —Chevrolet ad, 1956

Driving to work or to the station, to the shopping center, country club, or PTA, the automobile became as much a part of daily life as the washing machine, television set, or backyard barbecue.

For the teenager, being able to drive was a matter of social life or death. Whether a hood who spent his time cruising up and down Main Street or a nice guy who merely wanted to take Babs to the sock hop, a teenager's life was lived in and with the car. Being grounded (without wheels) became the severest form of parental punishment. And any teen in mid-fifties suburbia who couldn't drive was automatically burdened with the label "nerd."

In the 1950s anything wonderful was called "dreamy." A handsome guy was a "dreamboat"; a girl, "dream bait"; and the most perfect car imaginable, a "dream car." Each manufacturer made dream cars and displayed them at auto shows like the GM Motorama. You couldn't buy one of these dream cars—loaded with gizmos and looking like a rocket ship on wheels —but the cars you *could* buy were said to be inspired by these futuristic prototypes. The LeSabre that GM paraded around the country in the early fifties was a convertible with a moisture-activated top that closed at the first drop of rain. While that particular feature never appeared in GM production models, the LeSabre's pointy double-thrust "Dagmar" bumpers (named after a well-endowed starlet) were soon grafted onto the Cadillac. Likewise, its fins soon became part of production cars. Each year the new models came closer to resembling the dream cars. And each year there were new dream cars to set standards for the future, which seemed to be approaching at an ever-faster rate.

> *Who says tomorrow never comes? You're looking at it!*
> —Plymouth ad, 1957

Introduction of the new cars was a yearly suspense drama. They were trucked out of Detroit covered with canvas so as not to reveal "top secret" designs. Weeks before the unveiling, telephoto spy shots and speculative drawings of the new cars were "leaked" to the press as appetizers. Then, with families in rec rooms all across the country crowded around the Philco Predicta, the curtain lifted on tomorrow. The hypnotic spell of the television tube added drama to the unveiling of the new models.

> *Ed Sullivan and Julia Meade are waiting. Then the show is on—*
> *. . . And, sparkling in homes across the nation is the new, in-comparably finer Lincoln for 1955.*
> —Lincoln ad, 1954

Nothing could be more detrimental to one's status than being caught in yesterday's car. Each year the conscientious consumer "moved up" to a new car—by definition, a better car. This ritual was encouraged by manufacturers, who consistently introduced more prestigious models as they dropped the economy Plain Janes from the line-up.

Cars grew bigger, longer, lower, wider, and more powerful. Design had long ago been abandoned for the sake of style. Kay Wister, writing in the New York *Journal American,* noted: "These days you can have as much fun shopping for a car as you do shopping for a dress or living room curtains." She warned that "yesterday's car in 'a good neutral color' looks very old fashioned. Today, buying a car that looks exactly like Mrs. Jones' is in the same category as buying a dress identical to hers." Ads offered to women the opportunity to be "Chevy chic" and to match their new autos' interior to their own fashion ensembles.

One car was hardly enough, so new markets were created for "second cars." The new Corvette was "for experts only." The DeSoto with wide doors was "wonderful for party dresses and tight skirts." And there was Dodge's infamous LaFemme—a special model in pink and charcoal gray with matching pink umbrella and pink purse rack as standard equipment. Designed for the ladies, LaFemme became the favorite car of pimps all over the country. "Our object," a modern GM president proclaimed, "is not only a car for every purse and purpose, but, you might say a car for every purse, purpose and person."

The 1950s was the heyday of motivational research. Once again

Freud's theories were popularized, and the use of sex in advertising became the talk of every cocktail party. Maidenform offered $10,000 prizes to people who came up with dream situations for bra ads. ("I dreamed I stopped traffic in my Maidenform Bra.") Psychiatrist Jean Rosenbaum spelled out the phallic symbolism of the auto in the book *Is Your Volkswagen a Sex Symbol?* General Motors, who made the biggest cars during the 1950s, came up with ads in which the perspective showed virtual Lilliputians (usually women) admiring or caressing gigantic cars. The upswept rear ends of Chrysler Corporation cars were called "feminine" and deemed by experts on the subconscious to be "invitations to copulate."

Almost every car maker developed a pillar-less four-door hardtop. Vance Packard reported that this was a result of motivational research which showed that although men bought sedans, they were more attracted to convertibles. Just as a man might have a fling with a glamorous woman but marry the plain and practical one, MR people deduced, so he might want the convertible but wind up with the sedan. The hardtop, with its wide-open convertible look, was a union of wife and mistress, and became the most popular body style of the decade.

The hardtop was sexy—naughty but nice. Like Elvis Presley, who drove teens crazy with his racy gyrations but was still polite to his mom, and like the new magazine *Playboy*, which offered nudes to ogle but balanced them with fiction and "philosophy," the "sporty-looking" cars of the 1950s were still practical, respectable, and fit for suburban driveways.

*It's a tiger—but an obedient tiger.*

—Corvette ad, 1954

As early as the first Cadillac fin in 1948, GM stylist Harley Earl had linked auto styling to the airplane look, and nuances of aeronautical and aerospace motifs appeared gradually through the beginning of the 1950s. The 1950 Nash Airflyte featured a "Uniscope" pod over the steering wheel. The Oldsmobile wheel had the planet Saturn and a rocket ship embossed in its center. Chrome side pieces gradually assumed rocket-ship shapes. Hood ornaments looked more and more like spacecraft. By the time the Russians launched Sputnik in 1957, Americans were thoroughly acquainted with the symbolic emblems of space travel.

The big leap into outer space began in 1955 with the new line of Chrysler Corporation cars. Designed by Virgil Exner (who by the end of the decade was nicknamed Virgil Excess), the cars were said to feature "the forward look." Then came "flight-sweep styling." And in 1957 Exner put fins on the Chrysler line that topped even the wildest dream cars. They were advertised as "cars that can do what they look like they can do" (fly to Mars?). The great fin war was on, and between 1957 and 1960 automobile styling entered its most baroque phase. Advertising copywriters fanned the flames:

> *It tames a tornado of torque. It breaks through the vibration barrier. It is swept-wing mastery of motion. It unleashes a hurricane of power! Autodynamics has unleashed the thundering power of a new aircraft-type V-8 engine.*
>
> —Dodge ad, 1957

The 1958 Buick was dubbed the Airborne B-58 (after the bomber). Its engine became the B-12000 because it developed twelve thousand pounds of thrust behind every piston stroke. It had air-poise suspension and Flight-pitch Dynaflow. Presumably to keep it from taking off, it featured an all-time record load of forty-four pounds of chrome-trim ballast.

Yes, the 1950s were a skyward-looking decade. Men from Mars and UFOs rode through popular fantasies in anticipation of the real space travel that the future promised. But few alien vehicles could match the Edsel for bizarre looks or for the hostile reception it received. It was conceived in the spirit of Detroit's most frenzied period of sculpted steel, applied chrome, and mannerist distortion. It came out (in late 1957) as an economic slump set in, and as the excesses of Detroit began to look decadent. By 1959, automobile styling had become the butt of jokes. Edsel took the brunt, described as everything from "an Oldsmobile sucking a lemon" (by Jack Parr) to "Utopian Turtletop" (by poetess Marianne Moore). And much worse. Today, to call something an Edsel is to condemn it as a catastrophic flop.

A strain of cynicism had begun to infect the once optimistically motorized nation. The year of the Edsel was the same year Herbert Stempel told the New York District Attorney that the popular TV show *Twenty One* was fixed, breaking open a quiz-show scandal that reverberated beyond the television set. Sick humor was at a peak.

The design advances and "look of tomorrow" trumpeted with the introduction of every new automobile were beginning to look more like fads than future, just more hula hoops spun out by the stylists. Nothing aged faster than last year's fin.

Car ads looked as overinflated as the cars themselves. Buyers were no longer rushing to the showroom at the promise of "Revolutionary new, nothing-like-it Turboglide with Triple-Turbine Take-Off!" (Chevrolet ad, 1958). The year 1959 saw the introduction of Detroit's compact cars. And the one car with sales figures that had consistently gone up through the 1950s began to advertise. It didn't promise a dream life or rocket-ship ride. It suggested that the car buyer "think small."

FRYERS
FRESH
EGGS
COTTAGE CHEESE

HONEY

CIDER
VINEGAR

CHEVROLET

American as cider in the fall,
Reliable as the good earth,
Familiar as a roadside stand,
That's Chevrolet—America's favorite car!

1951

**335-Horsepower Performance from a 550-Pound Motor**— GM engineers developed an entirely new light alloy engine for these cars. It is a V-8, with 10 to 1 compression ratio, supercharged by a blower developed by GM engineers for Diesel engines. Operates on premium-grade fuel at normal speeds—premium fuel plus special fuel at higher speeds.

# How GM engineers explore new horizons

Here you see the XP-300 and Le Sabre. The press likes to call them "cars of the future." Thousands of people have flocked to see them, and the question most often asked is, "When will you build cars like these for the public?"

Well, the answer is — these aren't intended to show exactly what future cars will be like. They were built and rebuilt over a period of several years, to give our engineers and designers the chance to test out fresh and forward ideas, and get these ideas beyond the blueprint and laboratory stage.

You never know, till you get far-in-advance ideas to the point where you can road-test them and let folks look at them, how practical they'll be—and how the public will take them.

Many of today's commonplace features came right out of "tries" like these. And as time goes on, some of these advance features are sure to appear on cars in regular production.

Le Sabre and XP-300 are just the latest examples of how far we go to make the key to a GM car your key to greater value.

*Your Key to Greater Value—the Key to a General Motors Car*

## GENERAL MOTORS
"MORE AND BETTER THINGS FOR MORE PEOPLE"

CHEVROLET · PONTIAC · OLDSMOBILE
BUICK · CADILLAC · BODY BY FISHER
GMC TRUCK & COACH

**The Top that's Worked by a Raindrop**—Rain falling on sensitized spot between Le Sabre seats starts mechanism which raises and locks top, rolls up side windows. Steering post and seats of XP-300 are vertically adjustable to person's height. Contour seat backs can be moved forward at belt line to ease back strain. Both cars have built-in jacks for easy tire changing.

# You don't have to "just look" at this dream car... <u>YOU CAN OWN IT NOW!</u>

# THE CHEVROLET CORVETTE

It's in volume production and on its way to Chevrolet dealers all over the country! The dashing Corvette stands only 33 inches at door top—has an overall length of 167 inches on a 102-inch wheelbase. It has outrigger type rear springs and a wide 57-inch front wheel tread for true sports car roadability. A special 150-horsepower "Blue-Flame" high-compression engine with three carburetors gives you thrilling performance. Service and parts are always as close as your nearest Chevrolet dealer. Drop in soon and let him put you behind the wheel of America's number one fun car!... Chevrolet Division of General Motors, Detroit 2, Michigan.

**First of the dream cars to come true**

# Child of the magnificent ghosts

Years ago this land knew cars that were fabricated out of sheer excitement. Magnificent cars that uttered flame and rolling thunder from exhaust pipes as big around as your forearm, and came towering down through the summer dust of American roads like the Day of Judgment.

They were the sports cars in a day when all motoring was an adventure, and no man who ever saw one can forget the flare of sun on brass, the brave colors and the whirlwind of their passage.

They have been ghosts for forty years, but their magic has never died. And so, today, they have an inheritor — for the Chevrolet Corvette reflects, in modern guise, the splendor of their breed.

It is what *they* were: a vehicle designed for the pure pleasure of road travel. It handles with a precision that cannot be duplicated by larger cars — and it whistles through curves as though it were running on rails.

You can watch a Corvette in action and imagine some of the elation it offers. But you have to put your own hands on that husky steering wheel to taste the full pleasure of really *controlling* a car.

Who can tell you about the cyclone sound of that 195-horsepower V8 engine, or the fantastic surge of acceleration that answers an ounce of throttle pressure? Who can describe the wonderful feeling of confidence and relaxation that stems from true sports car roadability, or the genuine astonishment that comes when you first tap those rock-solid brakes?

Who can make you feel what it is like to drive a car that always has more on hand — in road-holding, acceleration, stopping power — than you'll virtually ever use? You'll have to try it for yourself. And when you drop in at your Chevrolet dealer's, he'll take particular pride in showing you the car that is a true child of those magnificent ghosts — the V8 Corvette! . . . Chevrolet Division of General Motors, Detroit 2, Michigan.

## CHEVROLET CORVETTE

## "This my wife would never understand"

"Well, it was like this. I was the sort who knew his own mind, knew what he wanted. Didn't ask advice often, particularly at home. Seeing that beauty on the street was what woke me up to what I'd been missing. Here I'd been buying the same old kind of car, year after year, never asking the little woman what she wanted. Man, that Aero Willys made me realize that something's happened in the automobile business. When I saw that car, and realized how beautiful it was . . . how it was made by Willys Motors who made the 'Jeep' famous . . . I determined to buy an Aero Willys for my wife. It wasn't even her birthday, (and I don't think it was an anniversary of any kind) that's why she can't understand it. But is she happy with her new **AERO WILLYS**"

TO UNDERSTANDING HUSBANDS:
Escort your wife to a Willys show-room today. We'll do the rest!

© 1953, Willys Motors, Inc., Toledo

1953

**CHEVROLET**

*Companion of carefree days*

This could be yours—green knoll,
blue skies and all. This could be you,
far distant from a world of cares
. . . steeped in content.
The way's not hard to find
in a Chevrolet convertible. There's power aplenty
in its nimble, spirited Valve-in-Head engine,
and there's a choice of drives—
the new Powerglide automatic transmission with 105-h.p. engine*
or the famous Synchro-Mesh transmission
with improved standard Valve-in-Head engine.
And Body by Fisher—
long, singing lines and harmony in colors.
Also Center-Point steering
and hydraulic brakes with bonded brake linings.
All this is yours
in the Chevrolet convertible, the perfect pathfinder
. . . the ideal companion of carefree days.
Visit your Chevrolet dealer.

*Powerglide transmission with 105-h.p. engine
optional on De Luxe models at extra cost.

CHEVROLET MOTOR DIVISION, *General Motors Corporation,*
DETROIT 2, MICHIGAN

1950

# More people named Jones*
## own Chevrolets than any other car!

*(And their neighbors are keeping up with the Joneses!)*

\*Of course, we haven't actually counted all the Joneses. But it seems a safe guess. Because this year—as they have year after year—more people are buying Chevies. And 2 million more people own Chevrolets than any other car. The past, the present and the future look brightest for Chevrolet dealers!

YOU'LL PROFIT MOST WITH CHEVROLET—AMERICA'S
FOREMOST AUTOMOTIVE FRANCHISE

**CHEVRO**

## More people b
## than any c

Just take a look around you on any city street or open road, if you want to see how America rates its motor cars. Your own eyes will tell the same story that's down on record in official automobile registration figures.

You're sure to see more Chevrolets than any other make. For today, nearly a million and a half more people drive Chevrolets than any other car!

Never in motor car history has there been anything to match Chevrolet's record. America has taken Chevrolet into its heart, and made Chevrolet part of its life, in a way that no other car has been honored in modern times.

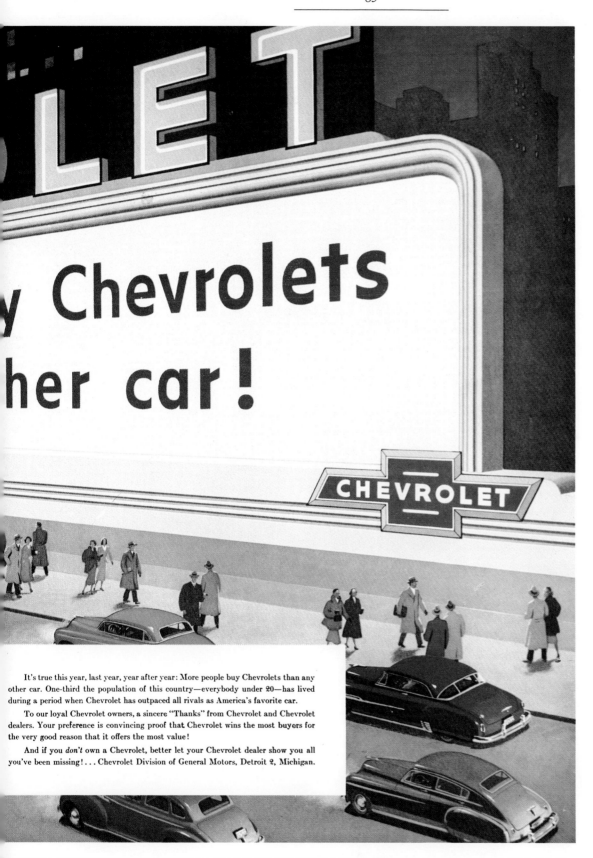

It's true this year, last year, year after year: More people buy Chevrolets than any other car. One-third the population of this country—everybody under 20—has lived during a period when Chevrolet has outpaced all rivals as America's favorite car.

To our loyal Chevrolet owners, a sincere "Thanks" from Chevrolet and Chevrolet dealers. Your preference is convincing proof that Chevrolet wins the most buyers for the very good reason that it offers the most value!

And if you *don't* own a Chevrolet, better let your Chevrolet dealer show you all you've been missing!...Chevrolet Division of General Motors, Detroit 2, Michigan.

*1951*

ABOUT CLOTHES AND CARS

## *You're going to Church*

It's a day of devotion . . . quiet and relaxing.

You'll wear your Sunday best—a beautifully simple dress.

Ride in fashionable serenity in a glamorous Motoramic Chevrolet

Bel Air four-door. *Here's why . . .*

**It's so inviting!** Kitten-soft foam-rubber cushions . . . lavish fabrics and trim . . . exciting colors . . . rich thick-pile carpeting. And lots more room for hats, hips and shoulders.

**At ease.** You ride in velvety comfort with new Glide-Ride Suspension—serene in your knowledge that it will cushion all road shocks, take you safely, smoothly, on your way.

**Sweep in and out** in ladylike fashion. The spacious and beautiful Body by Fisher is designed for graceful entrance and exit—seats are low . . . doors swing wide.

**You'll be proud** of the long, low, luxurious look of it. This sleek beauty makes fashion sense. It's the low-priced car with the high-priced look—the car most women love most!

## The Motoramic Chevrolet

*STEALING THE THUNDER FROM THE HIGH-PRICED CARS*

Chevrolet Division of General Motors, Detroit 2, Michigan

1955

# Every woman needs a *second* love!

A busy homemaker . . . and how she travels! School in the morning, the store, luncheon with friends, the church guild, school again and, perhaps, tea. And what makes hers the best taxi service you ever saw? Her second love —a car of her own.

And doesn't this smart new Chevrolet Bel Air convertible fill the bill handsomely? It's styled to turn the eye, and there's lots of room inside. Even the youngsters can't mar the bright two-tone vinyl upholstery.

She can see to drive and to park through the Sweep-Sight windshield. With its new low center of gravity, the car nestles right down on the road for safety and comfort, and Ball-Race steering even makes parking as easy as she always wanted it to be. Any one of four new engines gives her plenty of power when she needs it.

If the man in her life is extra good, she lets Chevrolet's extra-cost optional power assists take over, making driving as easy as she always knew it could be.

He's delighted, too. No more broken plans because he can't have the car, no more grocery stops on the way home. He has his new Bel Air sedan, she has her convertible. The price makes sense too. See your dealer. . . . Chevrolet Division of General Motors, Detroit 2, Michigan.

### The *motoramic* Chevrolet

*Stealing the thunder from the high-priced cars!*

# These carriers with

EARLY this week, a group of big automotive carriers cleared the yards of six giant U. S. plants and rolled out into the night.

Balling the jack. Because their steel racks held something they had never held before.

They were loaded with a new kind of car.

With four series—eighteen models—of a new kind of car called the Edsel.

And the delivery date is urgent.

covered cars are headed in your direction

The Edsel makes its public debut in September.

Maybe you'll see some of these carriers loaded with covered cars on your roads in the next few days.

If you do, you might call to mind what one of their drivers said before he started out. The driver lifted the cover on one of the Edsels in his load and looked it over very carefully. And what he said, plainly and forcibly, was:

"Man, would I like to have one of these."

# EDSEL

**New member of the Ford family of fine cars**
**See it at your Edsel Dealer on September 4**

EDSEL DIVISION · FORD MOTOR COMPANY · DEARBORN, MICHIGAN

1957

## DRAMATIC EDSEL STYLING is here to stay
### —bringing new distinction to American motoring

In one short year, the fresh and original individuality of Edsel styling has become a familiar part of everyday American life. Today, everyone recognizes the distinctive Edsel. And everyone who's driven an Edsel knows that Edsel *features* are out in front, too. Exclusive Teletouch Drive that lets you shift by a touch at the steering-wheel hub, Edsel's high-economy engines, new self-adjusting brakes and comfort-shaped contour seats are the biggest advances in years. Why not enjoy all these wonderful features—and drive the car with the advanced design—right now? Especially since there's less than fifty dollars difference between the magnificent new Edsel and V-8's in the Low-Priced Three!* See your Edsel Dealer about it this week.

EDSEL DIVISION • FORD MOTOR COMPANY

**Less than fifty dollars difference between Edsel and V-8's in the Low-Priced Three** *Based on comparison of manufacturers' suggested retail delivered prices.*

1956

# *This baby can flick its tail at anything on the road!*

DE SOTO DIVISION, CHRYSLER CORPORATION

DE SOTO FIREFLITE 4-DOOR SEDAN IN SEATONE BLUE AND WHITE

Take the wheel of a new De Soto. Pilot her out through traffic toward the open road. Before you turn your second corner, you'll know this is the most exciting car in the world today.

And here are the eight reasons why:

**New *Torsion-Aire* ride!** De Soto presents a new suspension that combines torsion bars and outrider springs. It gives you an exciting level ride, takes corners without lean or sway.

**New *TorqueFlite* transmission!** The most advanced transmission ever built, TorqueFlite gives you a smooth, continuous flow of power and exciting new getaway!

**New *Triple-Range* push-button control!** Simply touch a button of De Soto's new push-button control, and—like magic—you're on your way! Automatic with positive mechanical control.

**New *Flight Sweep* styling!** Here is the new shape of motion—long, upswept tail fins, low silhouette (only 4 feet, 7 inches high), plenty of head room, and 32% more windshield area!

**New super-powered V-8 engines!** '57 De Soto engines are rugged, efficient, and powerful! (Up to 295 horsepower!)

**New *4-Season* air conditioner!** This advanced unit—mounted out of the way under the dash—cools in summer, heats in winter.

**New advanced power features!** You can have your choice of the finest power features ever offered in an automobile!

**New glamorous interiors!** Each '57 De Soto interior has luxurious new fabrics with accenting trim and a flight-styled instrument panel.

Drive the 1957 De Soto before you decide on any car! You—and your pocketbook—will be glad you did!

**WIDE NEW PRICE RANGE . . . STARTS CLOSE TO THE LOWEST!**

**FIRESWEEP** – big-value newcomer for 1957 – priced just above the lowest. 245 hp.

**FIREDOME** – medium-priced pacemaker – exciting style and performance. 270 hp.

**FIREFLITE** – high-powered luxury for 1957 – the last word in design and power. 295 hp.

# DE SOTO

*. . . the most exciting car in the world today!*

De Soto dealers present **Groucho Marx** in "You Bet Your Life" on NBC radio and TV

1957

*This is your reward for the great Dodge advance—the daring new, dramatic new '56 Dodge.*

# The Magic Touch of Tomorrow!

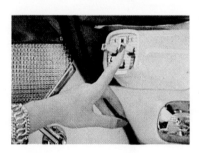

The *look* of success! The *feel* of success! The *power* of success!

They come to you in a dramatically beautiful, dynamically powered new Dodge that introduces the ease and safety of push-button driving —the Magic Touch of Tomorrow! It is a truly great value.

## New '56 DODGE

*VALUE LEADER OF THE FORWARD LOOK*

The new motoramic Chevrolet is a perfect mood-matcher. Anyone for tennis?

Going to town in perfect style—behind the wheel of a new Chevrolet.

And here's the new Chevrolet Bel Air Sport Coupe headed for spectator sports.

When something made by Chevrolet assumes a made-in-heaven setting!

The Bel Air Sport Coupe. You'll find your favorite model among Chevrolet's complete line of Fisher Body beauties.

*Little pink ears*
*From shore to shore,*
*Listen and sigh,*
*And ask for more . . .*

### Mesdemoiselles go for Chevrolet— everywhere they go *(and vice versa)*

What are the gals from coast to coast saying about the new Chevrolet?

That it's stealing the thunder from the high-priced cars?

That it's the leading fashion model in the world of wheels?

That it's got style all the while?

That it's hep, cool, or real gone?

That it's the one new car that's really lived up to its press clippings?

That it's the car they'd most like to be seen with?

That its new V8 engine, and those two new Sixes, give you more choice of power than you find in the New York Yankees?

That it does everything but the mambo—and with just about as much fun—since all the new power features available make driving it as dreamy as dancing with your best beau?

Uh huh—they say all that—*and more.* This new Chevrolet is a sure-fire go-for car. You'll go for it when you see and drive it.

And it'll go for you the way any smart gal likes to go when she goes places. Or something like that.

"See the U. S. A. in your Chevrolet" as our Dinah sings—and that means you, mademoiselle!

#### The Motoramic
# Chevrolet

*Stealing the Thunder from the High-Priced Cars!*

CHEVROLET DIVISION OF GENERAL MOTORS, DETROIT 2, MICHIGAN

CHEVY CHIC

Fashion's glamor is an end in itself. Rome's
Simonetta and Paris Castillo have
captured it in these lovely reflections of Chevrolet
style. Chevrolet colors—Simonetta,
with a short silk ball gown
in Chevy's Tropic Turquoise . . .
Castillo, with a daring cocktail dress featuring
billows of Arctic White peau de soie, a silk taffeta
bolero-with-stole in vivid Rio Red.
But in cars, beauty is only as beauty does.
That's why the lovely 1958 Chevrolet
is built to do just as you bid it. You'll
love its effortless steering behavior, its
obedient parking manners. See your
Chevrolet dealer for the key . . . . Chevrolet Division
of General Motors, Detroit 2, Michigan.

CHEVROLET

1958

*A dramatic portrayal* of the Body by Fisher in the 1958 Oldsmobile Ninety-Eight Holiday Coupe.

# The secret is in the build—
## THE NEW "SOUND BARRIER" BODY BY FISHER

Built to stay silent for years—that's the new "Sound Barrier" Body by Fisher.

Its secret? Life-Span Build — with roof structure, side members and steel foundation *integrally joined* into one unit.

Result: every Fisher Body shrugs off the shakes and shuts out road noises.

The new "Sound Barrier" Body is the latest achievement in 50 years of Fisher Body "firsts."

* * *

Another Fisher Body dividend: Safety Plate glass in every window—front, rear *and side!*

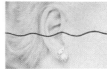

**HEARD THROUGH AN ELECTRONIC EAR.** On the left, you can "see" the annoying road noises as recorded by an oscilloscope in a '58 car body before the application of 23 "Sound Barrier" insulating and sealing materials. Compare that jagged "loud" line with the *subdued* sound waves recorded in a "Sound Barrier" Body by Fisher.

## Only the "GM Five" give you the Bonus of BODY BY FISHER

50 YEARS OF BODY BUILDING LEADERSHIP

CHEVROLET · PONTIAC · OLDSMOBILE · BUICK · CADILLAC

1958

# BLESS DE SOTO

## for making seats that let you step out like a lady!

What a relief to step out, instead of having to crawl out of your car. No more hiked-up skirts. No more popping runs. The '59 De Soto's new Sports Swivel Seats let anyone —tall or short—slip in or out in one easy motion.

Being a woman, you'll appreciate De Soto interiors, too. They're as smartly styled as your own living room. And everyone will like De Soto's magnificent ride... roominess...and power. See the fashion leader of the year at your De Soto dealer's today. Try the new Sports Swivel Seats yourself!

*The smart way to go places...* DE SOTO

1959

Out of the blue—

# the Big Break

IT'S THE NEW FACE OF FASHION—

THE NEW FEELING OF FLIGHT

## THE AIR BORN

We began with a clean sheet of paper and a dream that burned bright as a flame.

We wanted to give you a new kind of car—

A decisive break-through into a new era of transportation by land.

*We wanted to extend it to style, ride, performance, handling— to noise suppression, vibration elimination—to a completely new concept of motion. And to backbone it all with a new peak of precision manufacture beyond anything the automobile industry had ever reached before.*

When you drive the 1958 Buick, we believe you will agree we made that dream come true.

The B-12000 Engine— most advanced V8 engine possible to build for today's fuels.

# through

At the wheel of the B-58 Buick, you command a car born of more aircraft principles than any yet built. It begins with a greater use of aluminum, and goes on from there.

It sets you in front of the style parade with a fresh boldness that looks poised for flight.

It gives you domination of a Flight-Pitch Dynaflow* that catches the rest of the industry flat-footed.

It appoints you chief pilot of a B-12000 engine that justifies our quiet pride. Introduces you to a Miracle Ride—and you can have it with the added luxury of Buick Air-Poise Suspension.* Protects you with air-cooled aluminum brakes* plus more thrilling important gains than we ever made in a single year.

Your Buick dealer invites you to see the B-58—drive it, thrill to it— at the first opportunity. There's nothing like it.

BUICK *Division of* GENERAL MOTORS

*Flight-Pitch Dynaflow standard on LIMITED and ROADMASTER 75, optional at extra cost on other Series. Air-Poise Suspension optional at extra cost on all Series. Aluminum Brakes standard on all Series except SPECIAL.*

**Flight-Pitch Dynaflow**— Never before such beautiful response. Every tiny motion of your throttle toe makes an ingenious stator bite deeper into oil moving at 180 m.p.h. You switch the pitch a million ways, smoothly, <u>automatically</u>.

**Air-Cooled Aluminum Brakes**—Year's greatest braking advance. Aluminum drums shrug off heat. 45 radial fins give extra "air conditioning." More positive stopping. Easier stopping. Longer brake life, even in worst-traffic areas.

**Miracle Ride**—plus Buick **Air-Poise Suspension**— gives you the stability of Buick Rotoflow Torque-Tube Drive, the firmness of an X-member frame. Ride on gentle coil springs, or choose Buick's new Air-Poise Suspension—which floats you on 4 columns of air.

# B-58 BUICK

When better automobiles are built Buick will build them

*When better automobiles are built Buick will build them*

# Solid click on the TROJAN campus

We previewed the B-58 Buick at the University of Southern California — and drew a more enthusiastic turnout than a movie crew on location.

What sent the students the most was that new Miracle Ride, plus Air-Poise Suspension.*

They couldn't get over the way this Buick levels itself, no matter how heavy the load, or where you place it.

They marveled at the way the worst bumps and potholes seemed to disappear beneath the wheels.

And what brought the widest grins of glee was the way this big B-58 sailed up the winding canyon roads without a trace of slew or sway.

When we tallied up the comments, "It's the greatest!" was the mildest.

So — go see what the hubbub's all about, at your Buick dealer's now.

BUICK *Division of* GENERAL MOTORS

*Air-Poise Suspension optional at extra cost on all Series.*

TRY THE MIRACLE RIDE OF —

# THE AIR BORN B-58 BUICK

See TALES OF WELLS FARGO, Monday Nights, NBC-TV and THE PATRICE MUNSEL SHOW, Friday Nights, ABC-TV

Gowns for mother and daughter
created for Cadillac by Jane Derby

*One of the special delights which ladies find in Cadillac ownership is the pleasure of being a passenger. First of all, there is the sheer physical luxury of riding in a new Cadillac. The car is wondrously spacious and comfortable—and perfectly proportioned for complete freedom of movement. Then there is its enchanting interior beauty . . . the marvelous convenience of its appointments . . . its great smoothness of ride . . . and its marvelous quietness of operation. We invite you to visit your dealer soon—with the man of the house—and spend an hour in the passenger seat of a 1959 Cadillac. We know you will agree that it is the world's nicest place to sit.*

*Cadillac*

EVERY WINDOW OF EVERY CADILLAC IS SAFETY PLATE GLASS    CADILLAC MOTOR CAR DIVISION • GENERAL MOTORS CORPORATION

*1959*

# IMPERIAL

**THIS MAN COULDN'T HAVE DONE BETTER . . . AND HE KNOWS IT!**

He steps to the curb, dynamic and confident. He's a man who seems big, although after he has driven away you don't especially remember whether he was or not.

What you do remember is the strength of his personality, the way people went out of their way to speak to him. And the glances of approval he got when his car arrived.

It could only be one car — an Imperial. The car and the man are perfect complements — the man of substance and the most impressive car on the road today.

Imperial bespeaks power, leadership and good taste. It is designed for the man who is successful and doesn't have to prove it . . . for the man who doesn't seek prestige because he already has it.

Looking at an Imperial, riding in it, driving it . . . these things change your concept of fine car ownership. But you need more than money. Genuine good taste is a part of the purchase price. This is why the trend today, among the most critical and the most discriminating motorists in America, is definitely to Imperial.

Why not ask your Chrysler dealer for an appointment? He'll be glad to arrange one at your convenience.

**THE FINEST CAR AMERICA HAS YET PRODUCED**

1955

# GOOD TASTE IS NEVER EXTREME

Certain people have it. Certain things, as well—that sense of right-ness we call good taste. You recognize it at once when it is there.

It is there in the '59 Plymouth, in the look, the lines of a car deliberately designed with flair, and with restraint. For good taste is neither stodgy nor bizarre. It is not conspicuous. Nor is it anony-mous. It does stand out, yes—but handsomely.

This year, so many people of good taste are responding to the car fashioned most particularly for them—the '59 Plymouth.

*Plymouth*

today's best buy, tomorrow's best trade

Corvette Sting Ray Sport Coupe with eight standard safety features, including outside rearview mirror. Use it always before passing.

## The day she flew the coupe

What manner of woman is this, you ask, who stands in the midst of a mountain stream eating a peach?

Actually she's a normal everyday girl except that she and her husband own the Corvette Coupe in the background. (He's at work right now, wondering where he misplaced his car keys.)

The temptation, you see, was over-powering. They'd had the car a whole week now, and not once had he offered to let her drive. His excuse was that this, uh, was a big hairy sports car. Too much for a woman to handle: the trigger-quick steering, the independent rear suspension, the disc brakes—plus the 4-speed transmission and that 425-hp engine they had ordered—egad! He would teach her to drive it some weekend. So he said.

That's why she hid the keys, forc-ing him to seek public transporta-tion. Sure of his departure, she went to the garage, started the Corvette, and was off for the hills, soon upshifting and downshifting as smoothly as he His car. Hard to drive. What propaganda!

## '66 CORVETTE BY CHEVROLET
Chevrolet Division of General Motors, Detroit, Michigan

1966

# 1960  1970

*Help! I'm having an identity crisis.*

—LAPEL BUTTON, CIRCA 1962

The credibility gap had opened in Detroit long before it appeared in Washington. It was the dawning of the age of Aquarius, and the fat, chrome-encrusted cars of the late 1950s never looked sillier. They were "phony" and irrelevant. It was time now to be relevant, to "give a damn," and flowering from the lapels of the newly committed were bright buttons in support of everything from the miniskirt to the Maharishi, and everyone from Timothy Leary to Ho Chi Minh. But it would be a while before Detroit tried to "tell it like it is."

As early as 1958 *Look* magazine had asked, "Is the buying public tired of the big, luxurious 'living room on wheels' styling? Is a consumer revolt in the making?" To fend off the revolution, the Corvair, Falcon, and Valiant were introduced. The new compact economy cars sold well, but the auto makers' bet was hedged. Big cars sold even better. And in 1961 the "senior compacts" were introduced—they were a little bigger, a little more luxurious, and a little more powerful than the previous year's crop.

Detroit was beginning to offer the opportunity for just about anybody to "do their own thing" on four wheels. Autos became instant identity kits, each car's name an emblematic expression of where its driver "was at." For the person of leisure, there were "auto-resorts": Riviera, Bel Air, Malibu, Newport, and Monaco. For the hard-driving guy there were "auto race tracks": Bonneville, LeMans, GTO, and Grand Prix. You gave fair warning if you sat behind the formidable wheel of a Marauder, a Challenger, a Charger, or a Javelin. And heaven help the world if you were pilot of a Barracuda, Cutlass, Cobra, or Stingray.

Yet, with all these impressive Detroit identities to choose from, more and more buyers were becoming fascinated with the lowly Beetle. The VW was an anti-car by the standards of its day. It had no fins or carpeting or luxury features. It didn't get better-looking every year. It was, as *Popular Mechanics' Car Facts Book* said, "an honest car." VW advertising was built on the car's credibility. Qualities stressed in the ads were not the superficial and fickle promises of other cars but, rather, the solid, bedrock values. The Beetle was sincere. It was *real.* VW sales tripled during the 1960s and eventually fifteen million Beetles were sold in America, more than any other single make of car in history, including the Model T.

Dependability, durability, faithfulness, thriftiness, craftsmanship— Volkswagen ("the people's car") was to the sixties what the Model T had been to the teens—a beloved, hard-working ugly duckling. Buying one was a way of going back to basics. And so it practically became a symbol for the generation that wanted to reverse the technological nightmare symbolized by Detroit and later, more frighteningly, by Vietnam. A Volkswagen bus, covered with daisies or psychedelic paint, meant you were part of the Woodstock generation. It could also mean you were an effete snob who believed in flower power and wanted to make love, not war.

At the end of the sixties, poet Judith Viorst wrote about some of her own (and the decade's) automatic assumptions in a poem called "When I Grow Up":

> *When I grow up I'll stop believing . . .*
> *That people who buy VWs and Volvos are intrinsically more humane than people who buy Lincoln Continentals.*

But meanwhile, what had happened to Detroit's economy cars? They had grown fast and were no longer compact. Infected with the virus of the late 1950s, they began to flaunt more and more weight. Now they could be had with V-8 engines, "four on the floor" shifts, and decorative "sport trim" packages. Introduced at first to "kill the Bug" (as one Ford ad actually commanded), the American compacts had now become an expression of what was called at the time "territorial imperative." As in Vietnam, things had escalated.

All those war babies from World War II were grown up and named collective man of the year by *Time* in 1967. The ones who weren't driving old Beetles or tripping in a flower-power bus bought the new breed of escalated sporty "compact" car with the "youthful" looks and performance. None was so famous as the Mustang, introduced at the New York World's

Fair in 1964. It made the covers of national magazines and its sales totaled 420,000 in six months. It was cheap ($2,368), but there was a list of fifty options you could get, including simulated wire wheel covers and "rally-pac." Most people bought the car "loaded" (which could almost double the price); and the Mustang grew, too, gaining six hundred pounds in the next seven years. By the end of its life (before the Mustang II) it had become a pouchy overweight caricature of its once sporty youth.

The Mustang was part of the phenomenon that became known as "the personal car." As the family unit underwent intense scrutiny and criticism, "family cars" became more and more symbolic of the pre-Aquarian age. Personal cars were made basically for two people, with only token space in the back for more. As the solitary twist replaced the palm-to-palm Lindy on the dance floor, so "the personal car" exchanged the physical contact of the bench seat for the more individualized comfort of the bucket.

Like the buttons that characterized the decade, the variety of available cars multiplied, so that virtually anyone could find one to express what was known as a life style. There were violent, aggressive muscle cars for hawks and hot rodders or anyone "into a power trip." For the more suave type with a Continental life style and maybe a dash of James Bond, there were the personal cars with a European flair—the Riviera, Toronado, and Grand Prix. For the hopelessly indulgent members of "the establishment," there was still the Cadillac, whose makers devised in 1964 the "mink test" for its cars. Women wearing mink coats would sit down, roll around and wiggle inside test-model Cadillacs. Upon getting out of the car, their coats were inspected to make sure Cadillac upholstery had not in any way disfigured the mink.

What about the "silent majority"? What about the guy who wasn't a hippie or James Bond or Attila the Hun? The guy who wasn't one of the new breed of singles, who still had a "nuclear family" instead of an "extended" or communal one? For him there was the all-American car, the Impala, by Chevrolet. Since its introduction in 1958 the Impala has outsold all other American cars except the Model T.

By the end of the sixties even the silent majority was just one of the many groups into which the Great Society had polarized. As much as Detroit tried to produce all things for every special-interest group, there was one they could not please—the consumer advocates, led by the archenemy of the auto industry, Ralph Nader. On January 1, 1964, seat belts became standard equipment. The same year Nader's *Unsafe at Any Speed* pointed an accusing finger at Detroit, singling out the Corvair as a flagrant example of the auto manufacturers' disregard for passenger safety. Soon after, the once-popular Corvair was dead.

The consumer movement was just part of the greater disillusionment with Detroit. The automobile became, for many, the symbol of American wastefulness, gluttony, and greed. Marshall McLuhan was predicting that the car's days were numbered, but that, like the horse, it would resurface in the entertainment field. It did appear in sixties pop art, in works by Wesselmann, Rauschenberg, and Edward Kienholz, and it now seems that McLuhan's prophecy has in part come true. The "horse opera" was replaced during the sixties by TV and movie "car operas," in which good and bad guys chase each other around for the duration of the show in automobiles.

People started doing funny things to cars during the 1960s. Not customizing, not even psychedelic painting, but whole recycling. In Trinidad, Colorado, "Drop City" was constructed from geodesic domes made from old auto tops. "Peter Rabbit [a Drop City resident] takes special pride in the community building," Barron Beshoar reported in 1967. " 'See that gold panel,' he says, 'that is from a gold Cadillac.' "

Detroit countered by introducing psychedelic color schemes ("Freudian gilt," "Anti-establishMint," etc.), mod interiors, and new personalities. You could buy a Rebel, a Rogue, and, in 1970, a Maverick. But it was too late. The battle lines had already been drawn. The Federal Trade Commission, the National Safety Act, and soon the Environmental Protection Agency were aligned with Ralph Nader, the consumer movement, and a small contingent of Volvo drivers with Eugene McCarthy stickers and daisies on the tailgate—all against Detroit.

When General Motors vice president John DeLorean resigned from his post in 1973, he said "the automobile industry has lost its masculinity."

In 1970 *Harper's Bazaar* asked a group of fifteen famous people what they would put in a time capsule of the 1960s; most included the pill, the miniskirt, a moon rock, long hair, and a Beatles record. A few mentioned napalm, an encounter group, the film *Easy Rider,* and the slogan "Black is beautiful." Some said "The decade's trips," but none thought to include a car.

turned
on

The young people of our world are turned on and tuned in to life. To its mood and music. To its adventure and excitement. And they're turned on in a real and honest way.

This tremendous vitality is evident in every minute of America's Junior Miss Pageant.

The girl who eventually captures the crown exemplifies the best that's in American youth—its fresh attractiveness, scholastic ability, performing talent, gracious charm, poise and assurance. This is much more than a beauty contest.

Chevrolet is proud to be a sponsor on this special occasion. It's one way we can show our gratitude to the young people of this generation for all they're contributing to make our nation great.

We hope you'll enjoy tonight's pageant.

**Putting you first, keeps us first.**

# Do you have the right kind of wife for it?

Can your wife bake her own bread?
Can she get a kid's leg stitched and not phone you at the office until it's all over?
Find something to talk about when the TV set goes on the blink?
Does she worry about the Bomb?
Make your neighbors' children wish that she were their mother?
Will she say "Yes" to a camping trip after 50 straight weeks of cooking?
Let your daughter keep a pet snake in the back yard?
Invite 13 people to dinner even though she only has service for 12?
Name a cat "Rover"?
Order escargots?
Live another year without furniture and take a trip to Europe instead?
Let you give up your job with a smile?
And mean it?
Congratulations.

## Dealer Name

The more of a stand-up-and-be-counted individualist you are the more you'll enjoy driving a Corvair

Corvair wasn't built for people who are willing to settle for humdrum driving in any way, shape or form. You get an inkling of this when you walk to the back of one, open up the trunk and find it full of engine. Or go up front, where all the other cars built in the U.S. have their engines, and find that full of luggage space. Or hop inside and find the floor virtually flat.

But the clincher comes out on the road when you feel how light and easy Corvair's rear-engine design makes the steering. How sure-gripping it makes the traction even in mud or snow. And how flat and solid Corvair's independent four-wheel suspension makes the ride.

Driving something like this is enough to satisfy the most discriminating individualist. But you really shouldn't put off getting down to your Chevrolet dealer's much longer. Otherwise it may look like you're just following the crowd.

**CORVAIR—Unusual the Chevrolet way**

CHEVROLET | GM

All that and new safety features, too, including two-speed windshield wipers. Use the top speed to cope with heavy rain or snow.

# Toronado.
# The all-car car
# for the
# all-man man.

The line of demarcation is drawn. Men on one side. Boys on the other. Cars fall into place. No question which side Toronado takes. Not with that brawny, broad-shouldered look. And that responsive performance from a 455-cubic-inch Rocket V-8, biggest ever built. And that masterful ride and handling, thanks to the superior traction of FRONT-WHEEL DRIVE and torsion-bar suspension. Like we say, Toronado is all man—right down to that man-sized trunk.

**The front-wheel-drive youngmobile from Oldsmobile.**

GM
MARK OF EXCELLENCE

1968

# С ЛЮБОВЬЮ ОТ М. Г.

(from MG with love)

"He pockets the Walther PPK, toes the accelerator and in seconds loses the Maserati in the convolutions of the Grande Corniche. Once again, MGB triumphs over SPECTRE . . . and every other marque in Europe!" There's a Double-O Section in this country, too: men who dream of action and excitement—and find it in MGB. Excitement in mastering the thoroughbred that thrashed all other GT entrants at Monte Carlo. Action in a 1798 c.c. engine (110 mph top) braced by an all-steel unit-construction body. Your MGB fairly begs to be driven hard and skillfully. No push-button job, this! Four-speed stick shift keeps you in control, up and down hill, mile after mile. Aviation disc brakes on the front wheels impose fast, fade-free stops. (Very useful when there are road-blocks.) Comfort? Convenience? Just look: English leather upholstery. Bucket seats. Snug space for two hangers-on in back. Padded dash. Trunk room. Tight-fitting convertible or stowaway top—take your choice. Economy? Low initial cost. Up to 30 mpg. Obstinate endurance. Invisible maintenance.
Pipe dream? Not at all. Your MG dealer wants you!

FOR OVERSEAS DELIVERY AND OTHER INFORMATION, WRITE: THE BRITISH MOTOR CORP./HAMBRO, INC., DEPT. T-26, 734 GRAND AVENUE, RIDGEFIELD, NEW JERSEY

**A most unusual car for people
who enjoy the unusual**

'66 Corvair Monza Convertible—with
outside rear-view mirror and back-up
lights among the safety assists that
are now standard equipment.

If you perked up when you turned to this page,
our research computer says you're probably
well informed, earn above average income and
have more or less "in" type tastes. That's the
kind of person who usually drives a Corvair.
But then you can't always go by research.
The fellow who turned all this up on our computer, for instance, was a frugal soul who read
nothing but technical stuff and drove the same black
sedan for 15 years. Then one day he showed up in a Corvair
convertible a shade redder than the one above. How did he square
this with his research? He didn't. That was the same day he asked
to be transferred to a job that would get him out on the road
more... driving his new Corvair.

**'66 Corvair by Chevrolet**
Chevrolet Division of General Motors, Detroit, Michigan

THE TOTAL PERFORMANCE MUSTANG HARDTOP

Life was just one diaper after another until Sarah got her new Mustang. Somehow Mustang's sensationally sophisticated looks, its standard-equipment luxuries (bucket seats, full carpeting, vinyl interior, chiffon-smooth, floor-mounted transmission) made everyday cares fade far, far into the background. Suddenly there was a new gleam in her husband's eye. (For the car? For Sarah? Both?) Now Sarah knows for sure: Mustangers have more fun!

Best year yet to go Ford
MUSTANG!
MUSTANG!
MUSTANG!

Tied down by today's car prices?
The Good Guys to the rescue with their "White Hat" Special.

What's a "White Hat" Special? It's a dazzling new Dodge Coronet 440—with the special features you have wanted at a special low package price! Listen to the list: your choice of a white or black vinyl top or a standard roof... deluxe wheel covers...white sidewall tires...bumper guards, front and rear...deluxe steering wheel...fender-mounted turn signals! Your choice of a 2-door hardtop (shown here) or a 4-door model! Colors? Choose again from a rainbow of nineteen! Air conditioning and V8 power? The Good Guys can make 'em yours for a breeze! Also, ask about the "White Hat" Special on Charger. Try a "White Hat" Special on for size. What more fitting way to join the Dodge Rebellion.

The Dodge Rebellion wants you!

  CHRYSLER MOTORS CORPORATION

*1967*

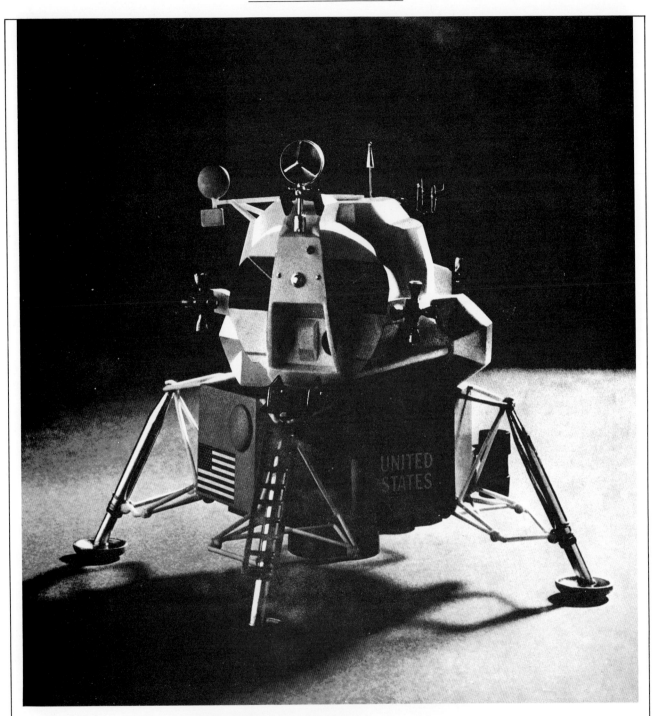

**It's ugly, but it gets you there.**

1969

**Datsun sets you free.**

Drive someplace new. Watch dust curl behind you on a country road. There's a good life waiting; it's not at all hard to find.

Surprisingly, many aspects of the energy crisis have made driving *more* pleasurable. Fewer traffic jams. Less frantic freeways. People are driving slower and enjoying it more.

When it comes to enhancing your own personal mobility, there isn't another car that fits the bill like a Datsun. It's sensibly sized and priced, and it saves gasoline. A machine for the times.

So, go ahead. Be free. Discover a new place, see new things, meet new people. Datsun's here to help.

Datsun Saves & *sets you free*

1974

# 1970  1980

The seventies were a time for guilt, apology, resignation, and recall. The operative mode in Detroit became the "modified limited hangout," a posture borrowed from Watergate. The auto industry was besieged: first came safety regulations, then a gas crisis, then inflation that virtually doubled cars' prices, then recall of millions of cars—all this accompanied by ever-louder beefs from the consumer movement.

Cars were "down-sized" and stripped of horsepower, and the speed limit was lowered to 55 mph. Federal bumper laws, roof-strength laws, padded roofs, and padded side moldings turned cars into anonymous shoe boxes on wheels.

The last convertible was made in 1976—a symbolic end to America's love affair with the auto. It had been deemed impractical—a fact that had never bothered anybody in earlier times. Convertibles had always been bought for the freedom they symbolized, and now that spirit was sacrificed for safety and sense. Cars of the seventies insulated drivers from the road. They became air-conditioned, soundproof travel capsules. Auto design had entered its orthopedic age.

Meanwhile, people were murdered trying to get gas during the energy crisis of 1974. America's car passions still burned. The killings were isolated incidents, but they were symptomatic of the desperation people felt when it suddenly looked as though the American auto was about to die of fuel starvation. Some people took their last gallon of gas and used it to immolate their Continental or Electra or Imperial. The gas shortage was countered by Detroit's "rebate" programs, which offered money up to $500 to anyone who would buy a gas guzzler. At the peak of panic you couldn't give one away.

The energy crisis passed, for the moment. Having weathered the storm, American motorists were asked to pamper themselves. "Feel good about your taste," a Chevrolet Monte Carlo ad reassured in 1975. "If your eye, your instinct, and even your bones tell you Monte Carlo satisfies your taste, trust them." Ford Motor Company, which did not "down-size" its full line for 1977–78, asserted that its still-jumbo Continental was for those who wanted to maintain their "standards." Luxury cars were designed by Bill Blass, Halston, and Pucci.

The indulgent car of the seventies was perfectly suited for what Tom Wolfe labeled "The Me Generation." It provided people with plenty of what Werner Erhardt called "personal space." Don't intellectualize, it said, don't be pressured by *them* telling you what car to buy. Trust your eye, your instinct, your bones. Assert yourself—you're O.K.—and so what if the Monte Carlo got well under fifteen miles per gallon of gas.

Another bit of pampering and self-indulgence was offered in the seventies when, magically, you could buy "the car you always wanted." The once expensive top-of-the-line Grand Prix and Thunderbird were rearranged in the line-up of models to be (relatively) cheap. They were touted as "classics" now offered for sale to the public en masse. "You owe it to yourself, you've waited long enough, you deserve the best," the ads were saying, offering the auto as a form of auto-massage. Implicit in this approach was a fundamental fatalism that whispered, "You better buy that snazzy, classy car *now* because pretty soon they're all going to be little, economical, government-designed safetymobiles."

> *When you buy a Buick you get more than a car. . . . You get a heritage.*
>
> —Buick brochure, 1978

Like so many Americans, cars sought out their roots for a sense of purpose and regeneration. Half-padded landau tops, opera windows, and the use of loose-fitting tufted upholstery all harked back to the craftsmanship of the classic coach builders. The 1978 Dodge Magnum was said to possess a "classic Cord-type grille," the Cordoba a "look untouched by time or fashion." In 1974 Corvette asked, "Have you noticed how legends tend to improve with time?" Classic nomenclature was dusted off and applied to new models, so that once again one could drive a "brougham," a "town car," a "cabriolet," or an "estate wagon."

It was a time of auto-nostalgia—for the "Happy Days" of the 1950s, the carefree cruising days of the popular film *American Graffiti*. Bands named Fleetwood Mac and Mink DeVille played music about drive-in movies and hot rodding around. Chuck Berry was exhumed to play *Maybeline* and *Airmobile* before a new generation of teenagers. In 1978 the International House of Pancakes offered a twenty-year-old Chevrolet as a sweepstakes prize!

The 1976 Eldorado convertible, "the last of a magnificent breed," became an instant collector's item. Every auto maker produced "limited edition" models aiming for prefab classicism. The inevitable energy crunch lent a "twilight of the gods" aura to these mannered offerings from Detroit.

Legendary, semilegendary, and just plain famous people lent their images to back up the mythology of the new cars' noble lineage. Douglas Fairbanks endorsed the Continental. Ricardo Montalban spoke exquisitely for Cordoba. Even Catherine Deneuve draped herself over the hood of a Mercury Monarch.

Auto ads "tied in" to other media phenomena to strengthen credibility. After the success of *Rocky*, Ford introduced its Fiesta and Pinto as "tough little street fighters that could go the distance." After *Star Wars*, more than one auto was shown flying through space (the rocket-powered promise of the fifties fulfilled!). Bill Cosby's persona—honest, down-home, trustworthy, socially aware—was enlisted to speak for Ford. And lest we forget, a once unknown Farrah Fawcett shared roof space with a Cougar for Mercury.

> *Baseball, hot dogs, apple pie . . . and Chevrolet.*
> —Chevrolet ad, 1977–78

All the nostalgia, root seeking, and star endorsements were part of what Riviera ads called "something to believe in" (1972). But lost innocence is hard to regain. After Watergate, full disclosure became the order of the day—especially so for Detroit after it was revealed that Oldsmobile had been sneaking Chevrolet engines into its cars while tooting the benefits of "Oldsmobile" craftsmanship.

Well, what could people really believe in? In the seventies natural was good, and so, along with Dr Pepper, yogurt, and "family style" cereal, many car ads went country. "Dodge is into pick-ups," one said, "like America's into jeans" (1977). "Chevrolet makes sense for America" appeared under rural landscapes and rustic country stores—the kinds of places, one assumed, in which a Chevrolet would feel at home.

Another aspect of full disclosure was the appearance in advertising of "frank talk," comparison tests, and, of course, mandatory EPA mileage figures. Designers and engineers themselves occasionally appeared. Some ads sported "blueprint style" lettering, suggesting the reader was privy to the car's careful planning. Ricardo Montalban even invited people to gaze upon the "Chrysler Styling Center." In some ways, it was back to the "nuts and bolts" advertising of earliest days.

Regardless of the halo self-consciously worn by the auto industry, car dealers consistently ranked at the bottom of the list of businessmen whom consumers trusted.

> *I have figured out the relation of advertising to truth. What advertising does to truth is what whipping does to cream.*
> —C. F. "Ket" Kettering, head of GM research during the thirties

From our own near-sighted vantage point toward the 1970s, it would be possible to interpret modern car advertising more as skimmed milk than cream. Where are the whipped-up peaks of the age of the tail fin or the smooth, organic formulations that came together in the streamlined thirties? Today's soupy maze of EPA figures, embarrassed full disclosure, and pseudo-classicism appears uniquely resistant to frothy whipping. Perhaps the auto has taken too many lumps. But if America is indeed falling out of love, the ads still pitch their woo. Whatever line they use and whatever techniques we see "up front" (to quote the seventies), there is no doubt they brilliantly mirror the character, the concerns, and the fantasies of the time. And that's the "bottom line" on auto ads.

I know. First you marry, move to the suburbs, and have 1.7 kids. *Then* you get a station wagon.

Well, I'm single. And I bought a Dasher wagon anyhow.

It's beautiful. The trunk has more space than the kitchen in my first apartment. Also more space than any wagon in its class, made by any manufacturer.

But then, Dasher is made by Volkswagen. So, it's hardly your garden variety wagon.

Dasher has what most wagons don't. Things like front-wheel drive and fuel injection.

# DASHER
## By Volkswagen

It's brilliant in traffic, moves like the devil on the open road, and sips its gas instead of guzzling it.*

I love my Dasher. Someday I may load it up with kids. For now, I love to load it up and take off.

*(EPA estimates, std. trans. 24 MPG city, 36 MPG highway. Mileage will vary depending on how and where you drive, optional equipment, and car's condition.)

# I bought a wagon out of wedlock.

1977

# "I don't drive the car for the prestige. I drive it for my own feelings of satisfaction." Robert Orr, D.O.

Dr. Robert C. Orr, osteopathic physician and surgeon in Detroit, Michigan, talks about how he feels about cars in general and Cadillacs in particular. He presently owns a Fleetwood Brougham.

"I like a big car. I like the style of the Fleetwood. I've had friends of mine who had Cadillacs mention that they are good riding cars, and I find this to be true. I believe in buying a big, substantial car that also has weight to it, because, on a trip I want to be in a car I feel comfortable in.

"I've had some long distance rides with the car and it's very satisfactory. I've been down to Florida with it, with the whole family in the car, and I couldn't expect a nicer trip.

"I don't drive the car for the prestige. I drive it for my own feelings of satisfaction. And there's another big factor, and that is I feel that a Cadillac is worth the price. To figure it out statistically, I'm in the car between 12 and 15% of my waking hours. And my feeling is that I want to drive a comfortable car."

On the question of age, he said, "I see no differentiation between a young person or an older person driving a Cadillac—whether it's a Fleetwood Brougham or an Eldorado."

Cadillac Motor Car Division

# FAT CARS DIE YOUNG!

(1966—1970)

Some cars destroy themselves in the mere act of carrying themselves around.

Burdened with tons of chrome and huge expanses of sheet metal, it doesn't take long for a car to collapse under the strain.

So in building a car that will live a long time, you must begin by acknowledging one basic fact. Fat on cars, as on people, can be fatal.

### VOLVO. THE FAT-FREE CAR.

When we designed the Volvo, a lot of superfluous stuff was dropped.

A Volvo doesn't have five feet of trunk hanging out behind the rear wheels. Instead of a long, low trunk, it has a short deep one. It holds more than a Lincoln.

Do you think your car has to be that wide? No. It's only that wide because a designer wanted it to look low. We make a Volvo wide *inside.* By curving the sides of the body, including the windows.

A Volvo doesn't need a six-foot hood because it doesn't need a gigantic gas-guzzling engine to push all the fat around.

We use a smaller engine, chop off the hood and move the wheels out to the corners of the car for better handling. Like on a racing car.

That way we can also make the passenger compartment bigger. And end up with more front leg room than a Cadillac. More rear leg room than the biggest Buick made.

### VOLVO LIVES!

Unfettered by fat, Volvos live to ripe old ages. We don't guarantee exactly how long that will be.

But we do know that 9 out of every 10 Volvos registered here in the last eleven years are still on the road.

If you don't believe us, look around. You can't miss an eleven year old Volvo. It looks a lot like a 1948 Ford.

Only not as fat. ⬤ **VOLVO**

1970